I0018539

Preface

The primary goal of this book is to provide AutoCAD practice exercises for beginners. This book contains 100 2D CAD exercises and 50 3D CAD exercises. Each exercise can be designed on any CAD software such as AutoCAD, SolidWorks, Catia, PTC Creo Parametric, Siemens NX, Autodesk Inventor, Solid Edge, DraftSight and other CAD programs. These exercises are designed to help you test out your basic CAD skills. Each exercise can be assigned separately. No exercise is a prerequisite for another. All dimensions are in mm.

✓ Click to download original 150 AutoCAD (DWG) files.

Disclaimer

The book contains 100 2D and 50 3D exercises to enable you practice what you learn. The exercises range from easy to expert level. These exercises are not tutorials. It is a practice book. You can use these exercises to improve your skills in any CAD software.

No part of this publication may be reproduced, stored in a retrieval system or transmitted in any form or
By any means electronic, mechanical, photocopying, recording or sold in whole or in part in any form, otherwise without the prior written Permission of the author or CADin360.com
All trademarks and registered trademarks appearing in this guide are the property of their respective owners.

✓ **Click to download original 150 AutoCAD (DWG) files.**

Acknowledgments

This book would not have been possible without a great deal of support. First, I would like to thank my parents for allowing me to realize my own potential. All the support they have provided me over the years was the greatest gift anyone has ever given me. Also, I need to thank Hira Nand Jha, who taught me the value of hard work and an education. Without him, I may never have gotten to where I am today. Next, I need to thank all the people who create such a good atmosphere.

2D EXERCISES

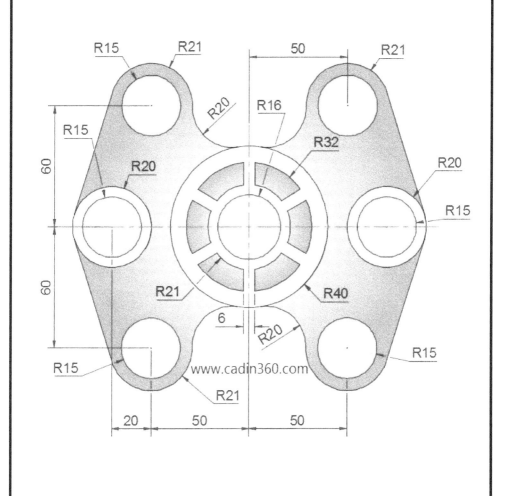

www.cadin360.com

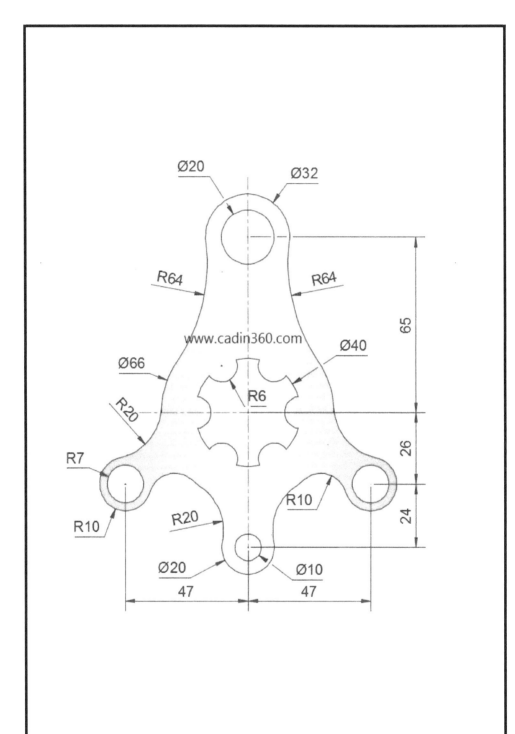

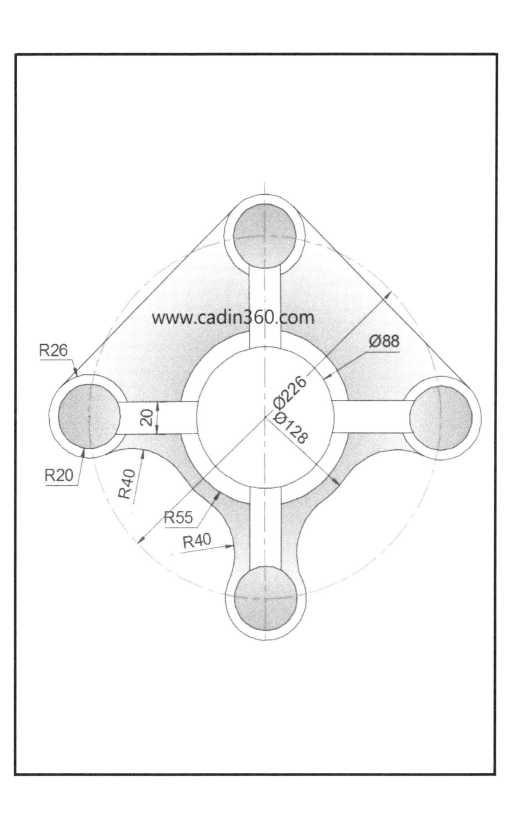

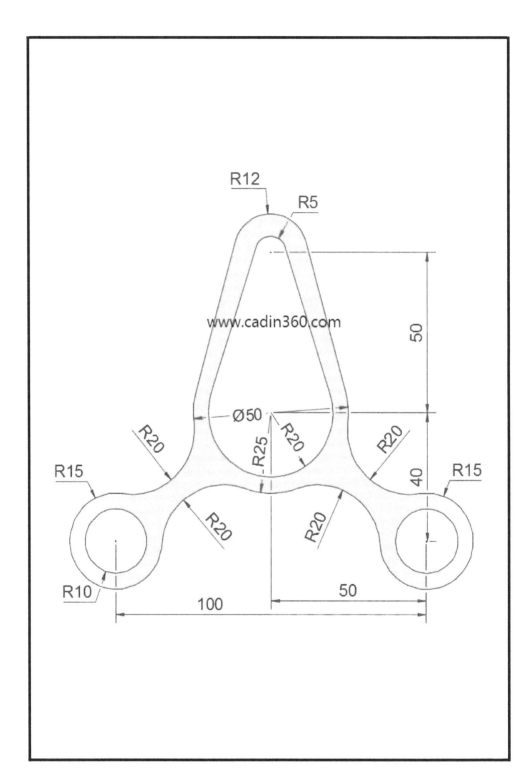

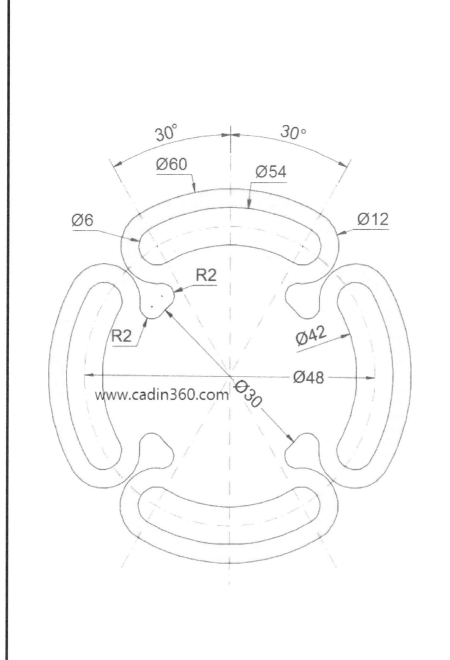

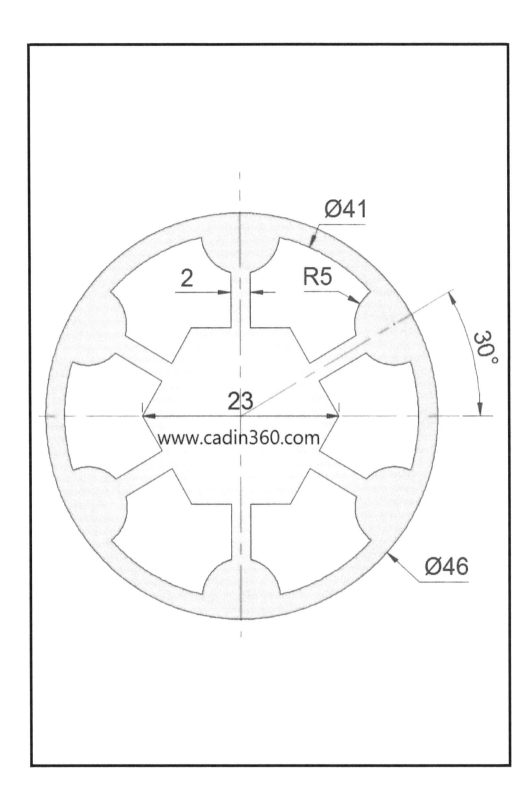

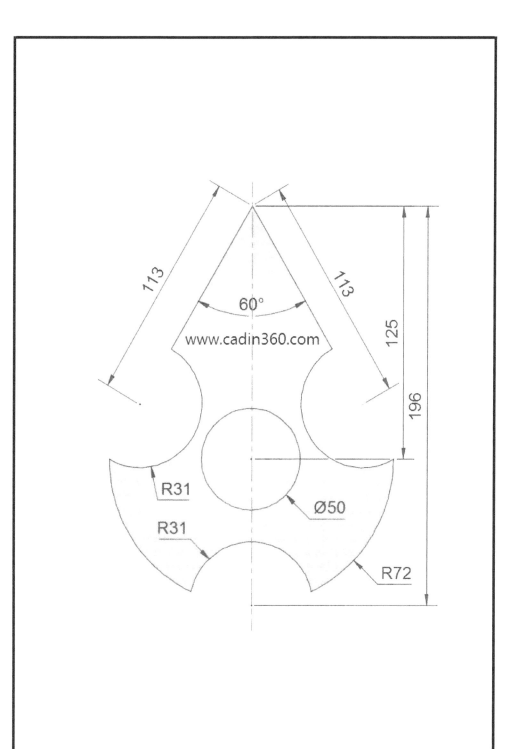

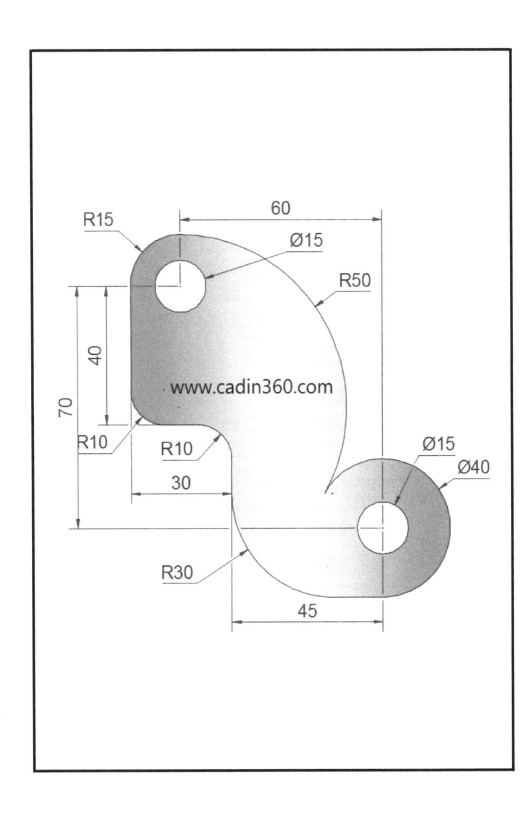

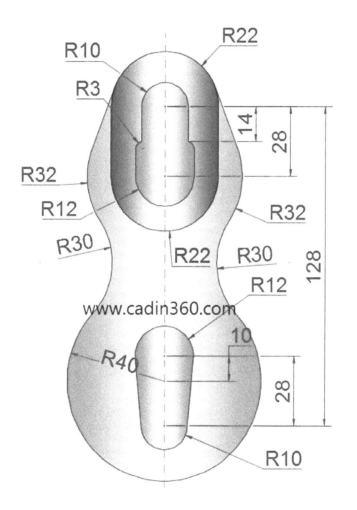

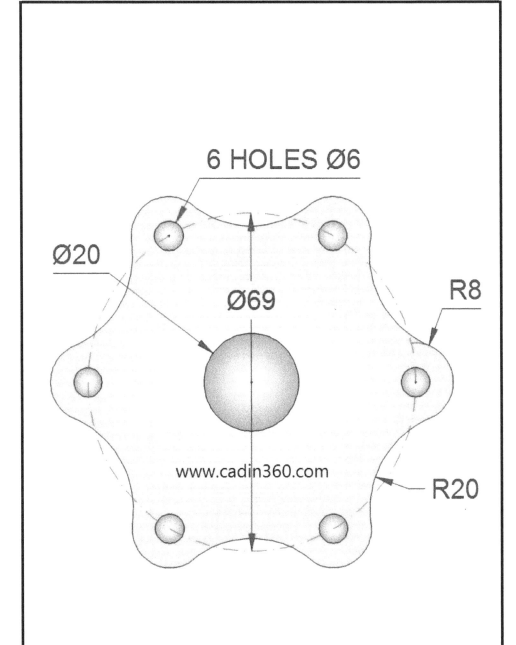

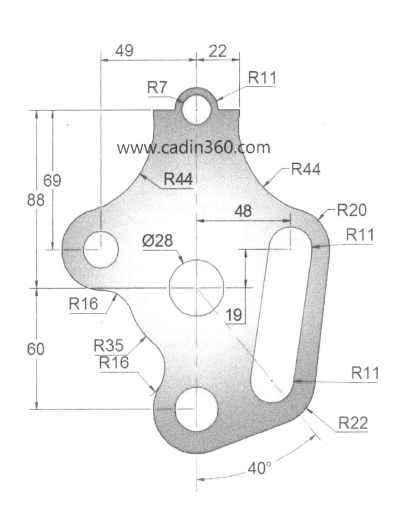

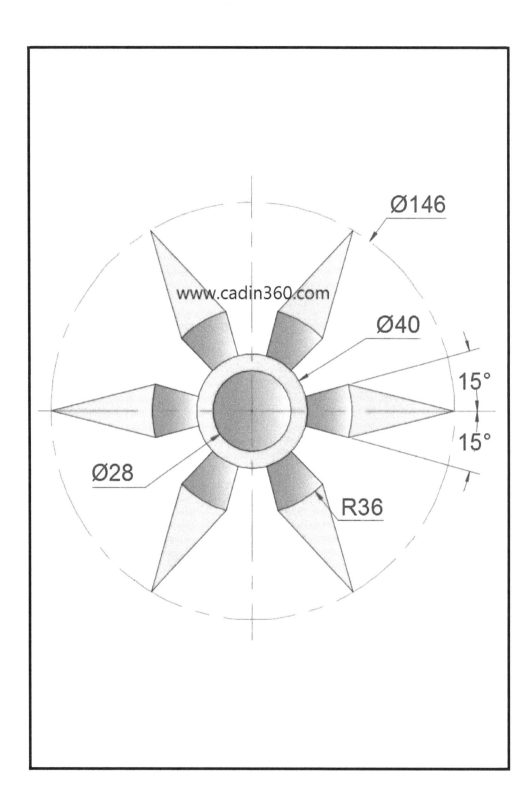

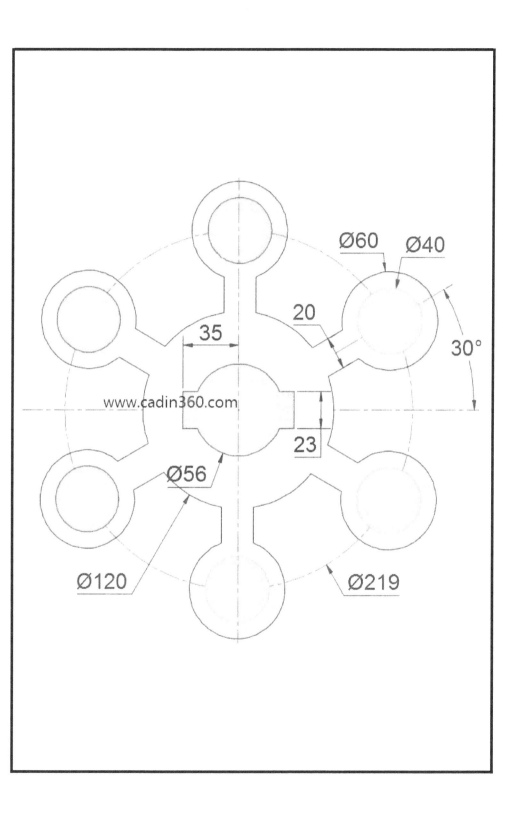

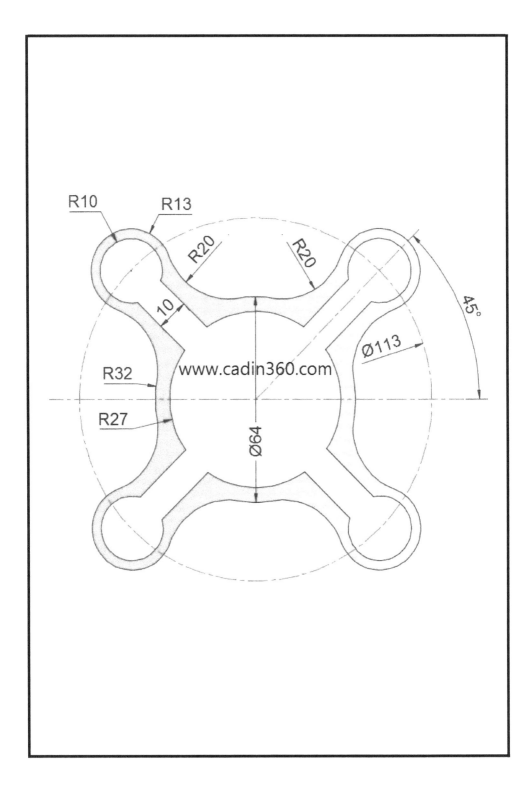

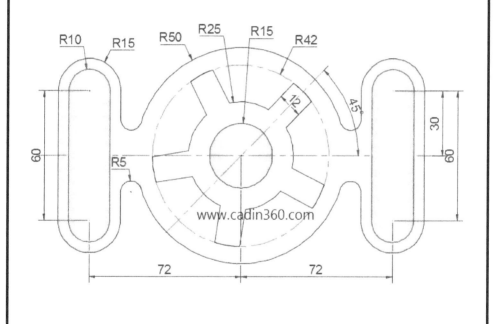

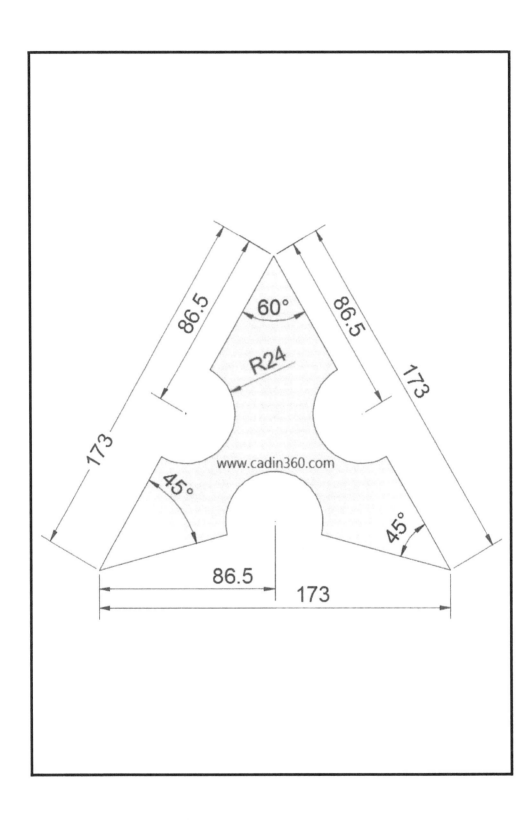

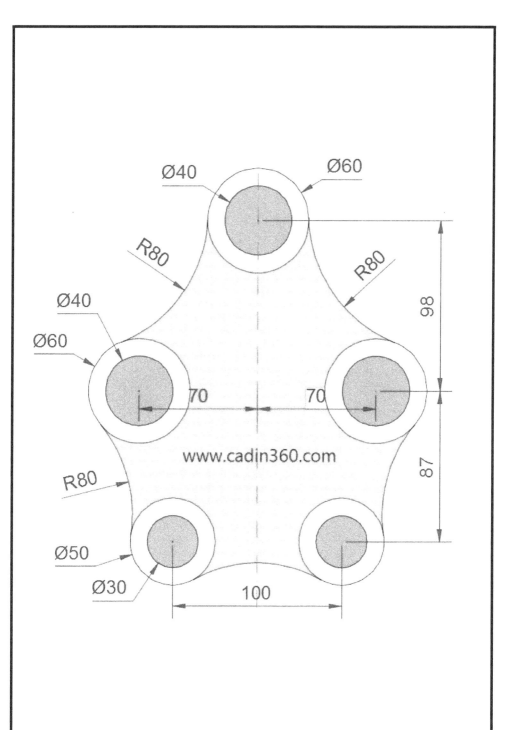

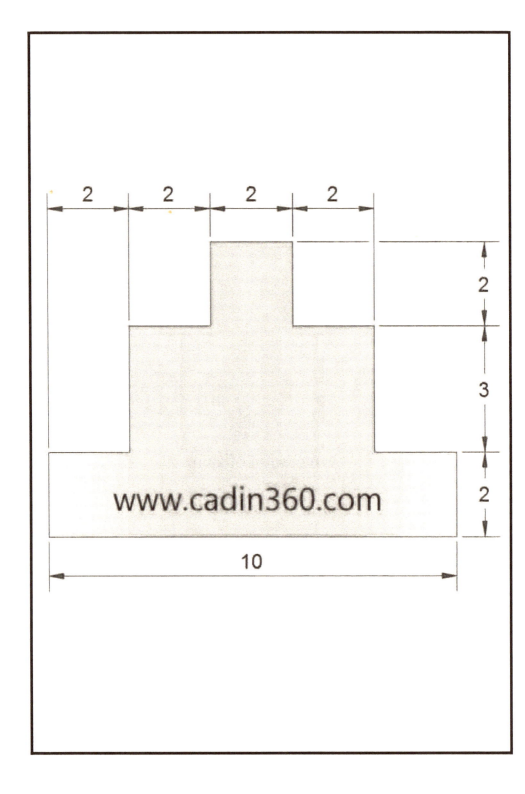

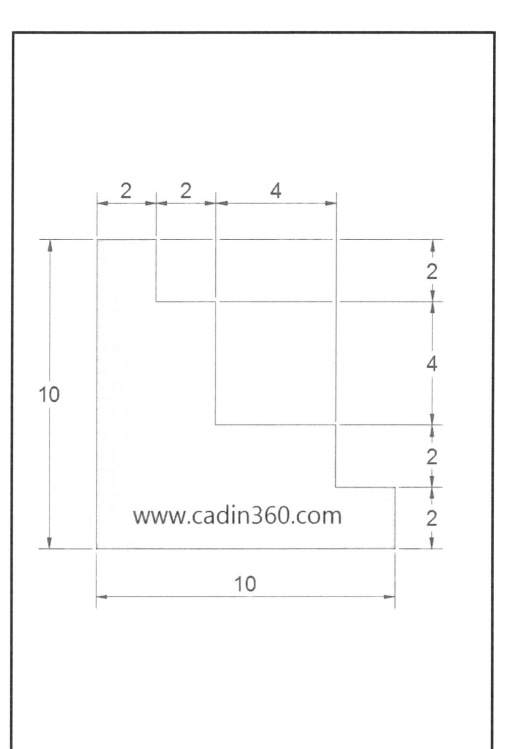

www.cadin360.com

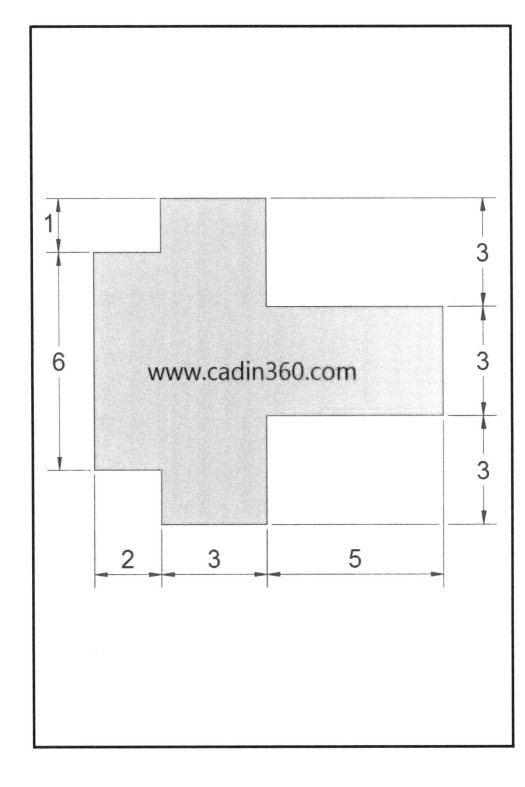

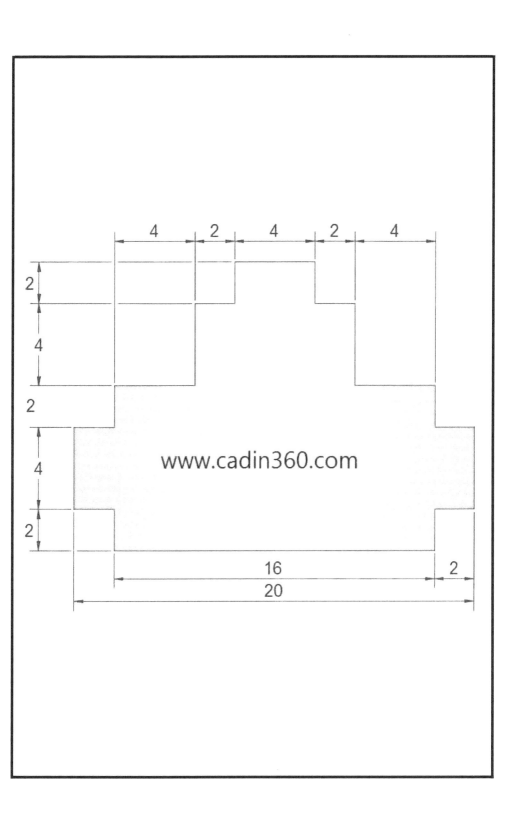

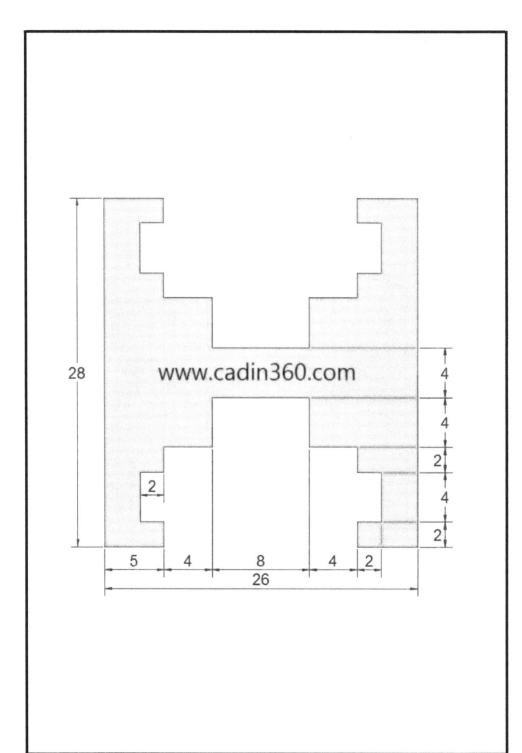

www.cadin360.com

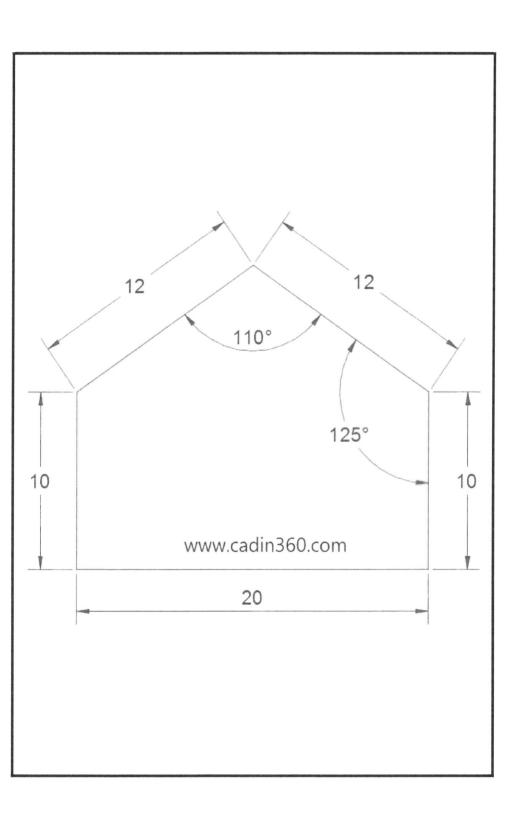

12

12

110°

125°

10

10

www.cadin360.com

20

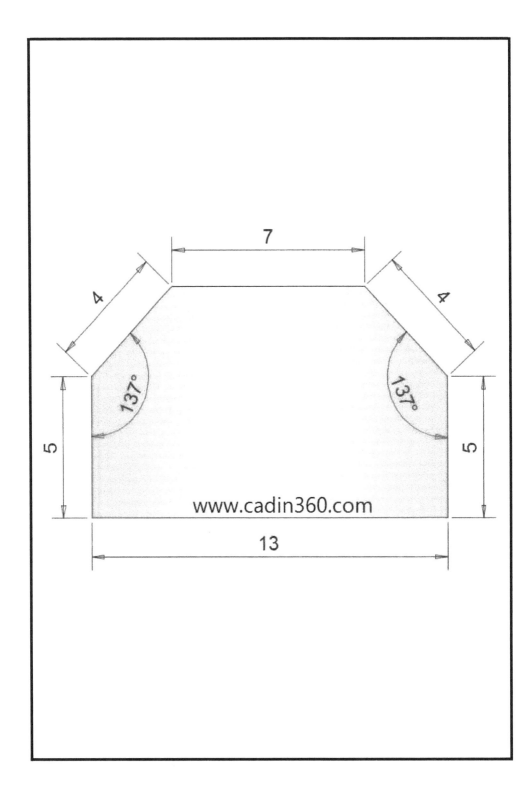

www.cadin360.com

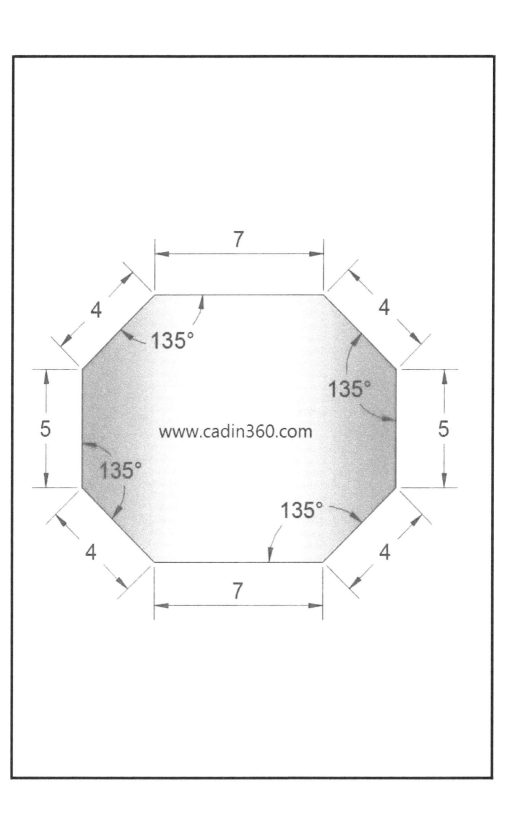

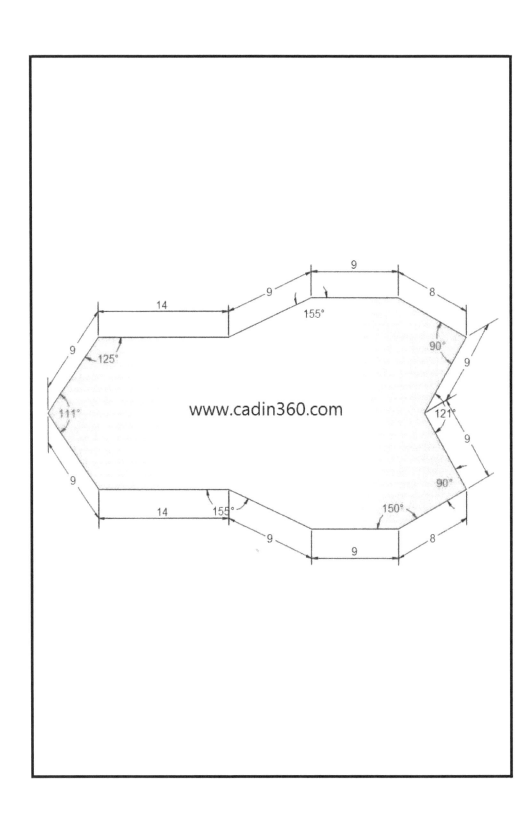

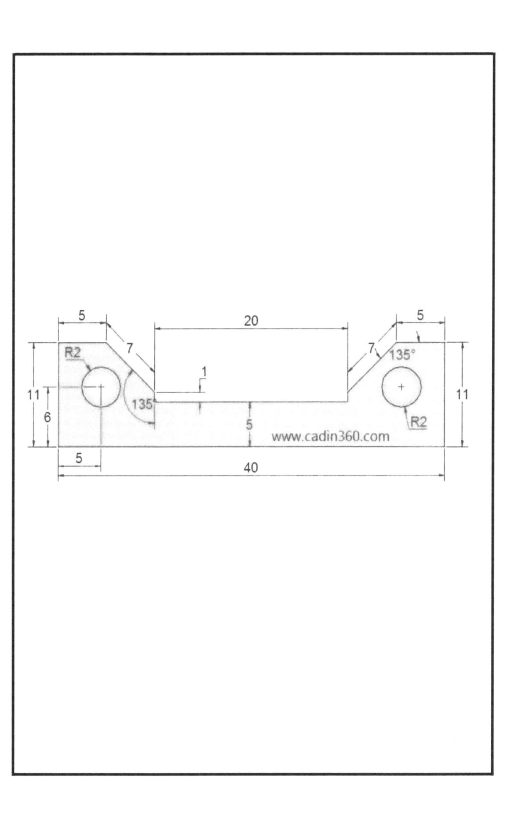

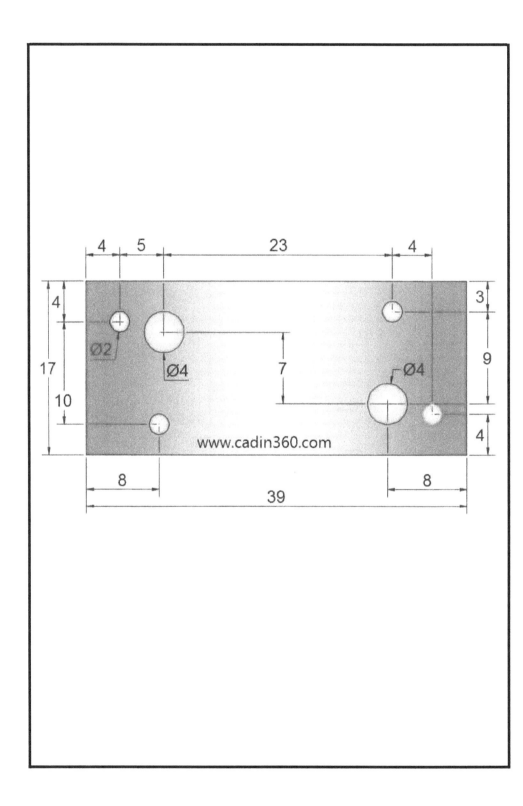

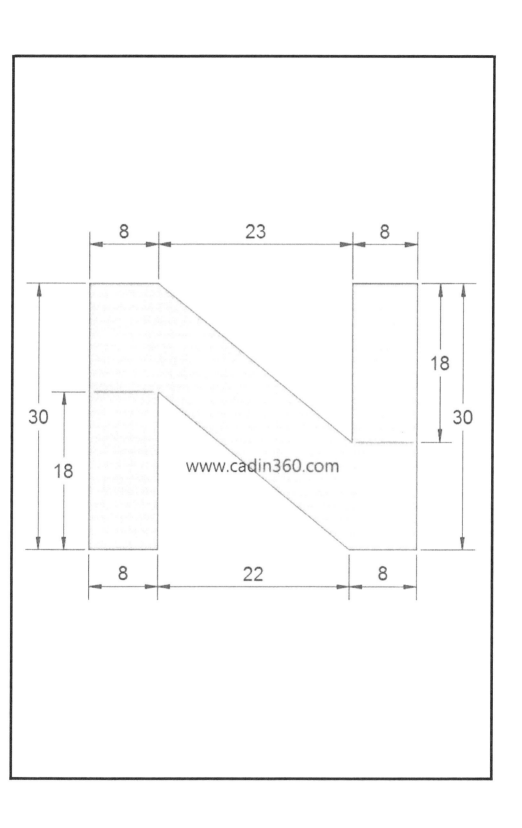

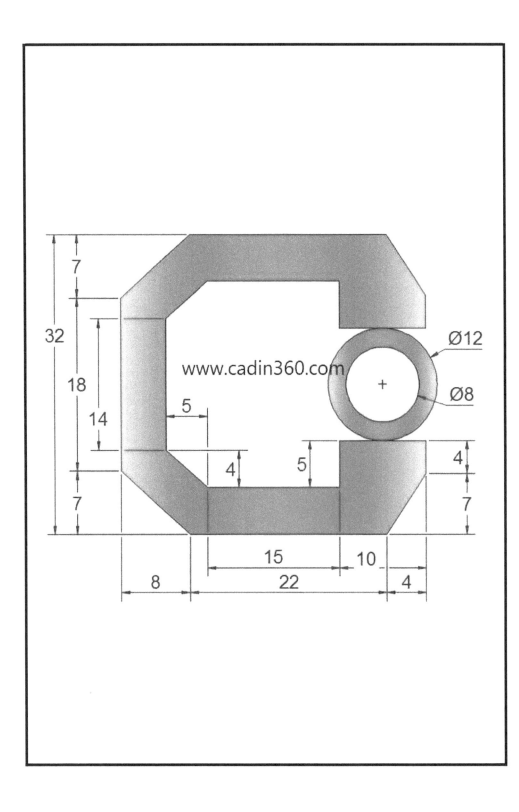

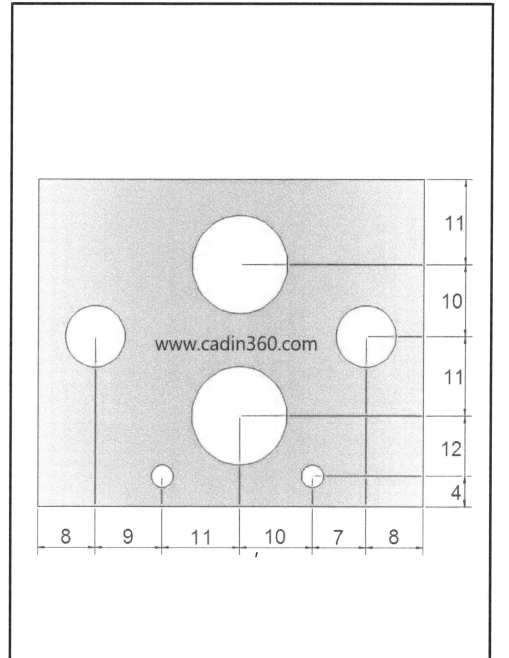

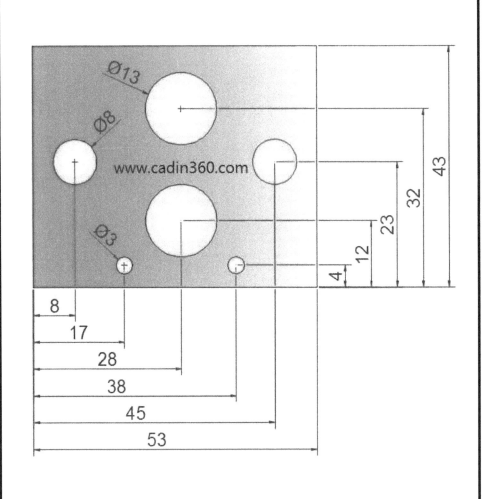

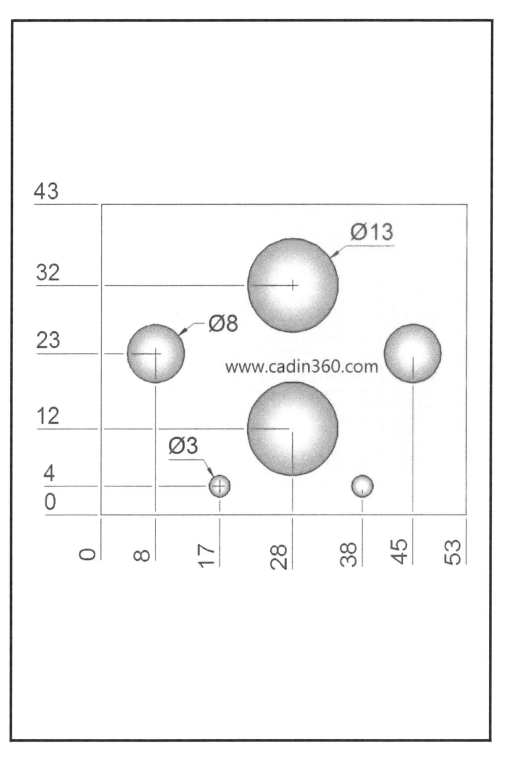

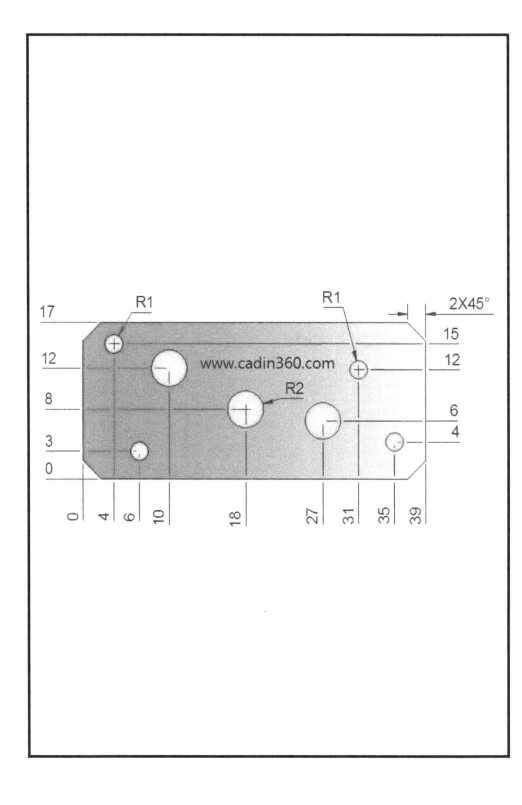

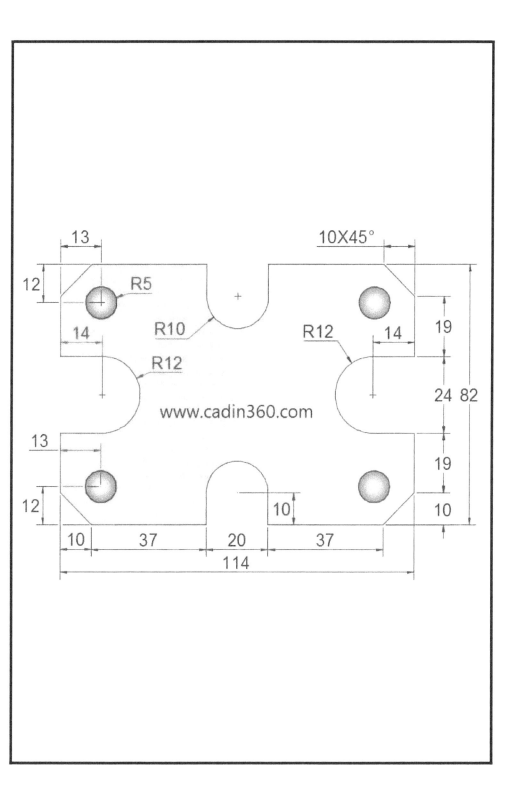

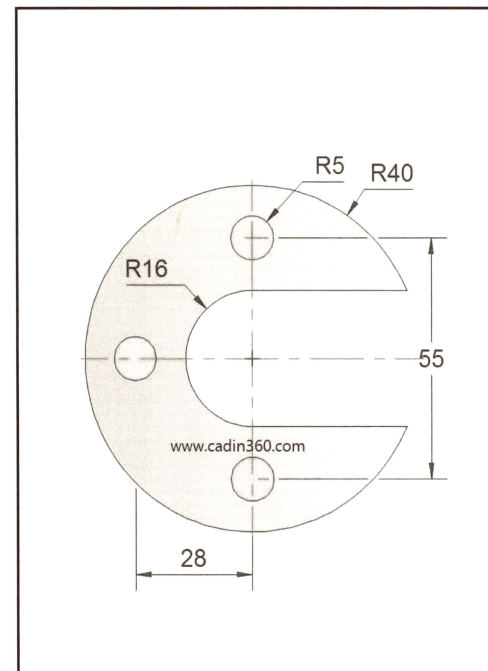

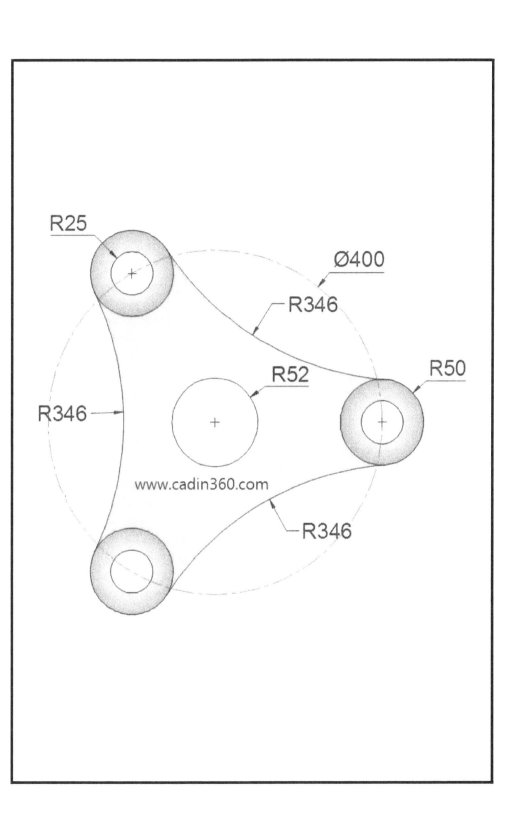

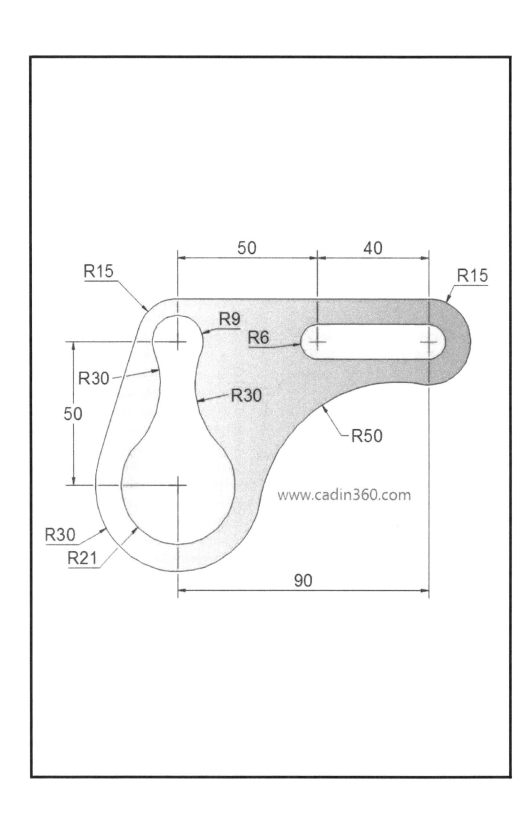

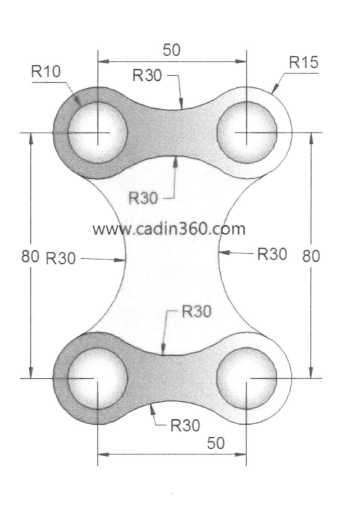

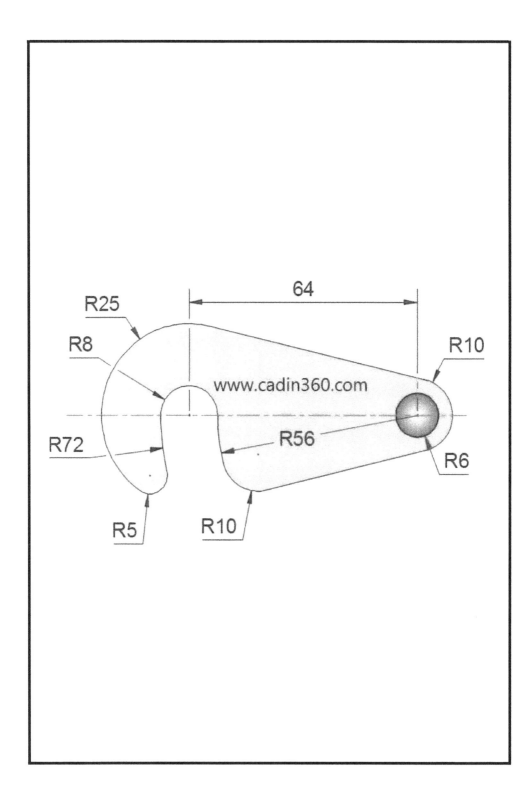

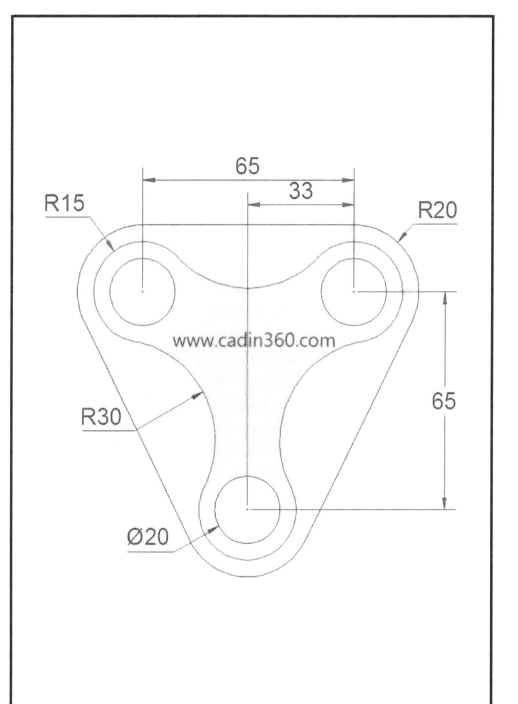

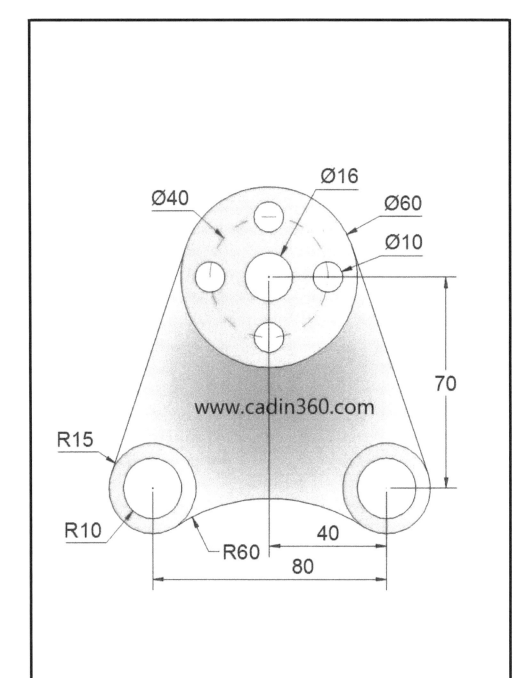

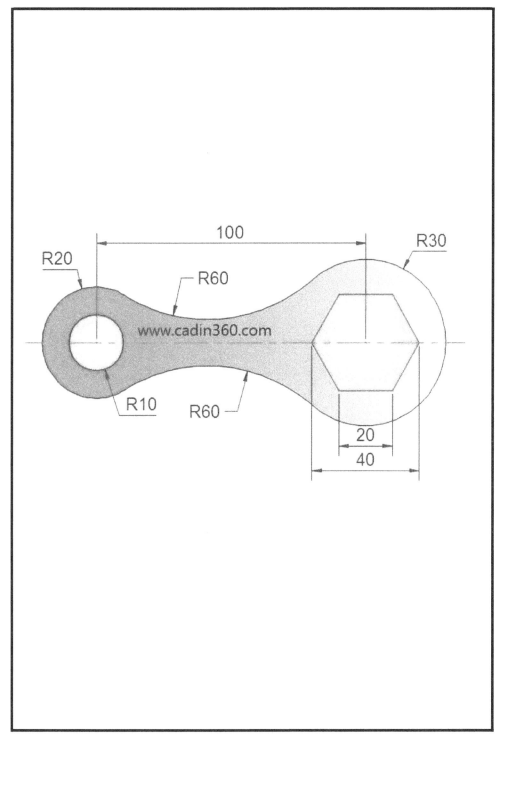

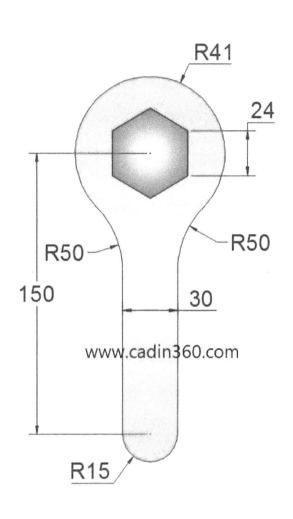

R41

24

R50

R50

150

30

www.cadin360.com

R15

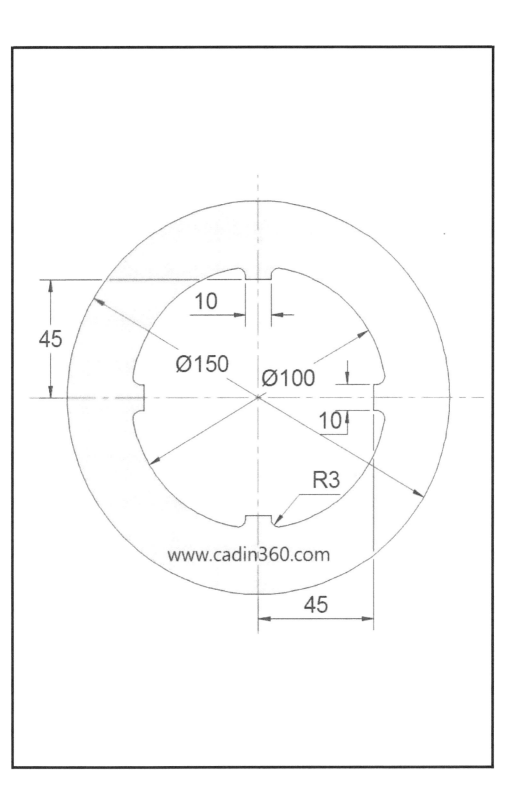

10

45

Ø150

Ø100

10

R3

www.cadin360.com

45

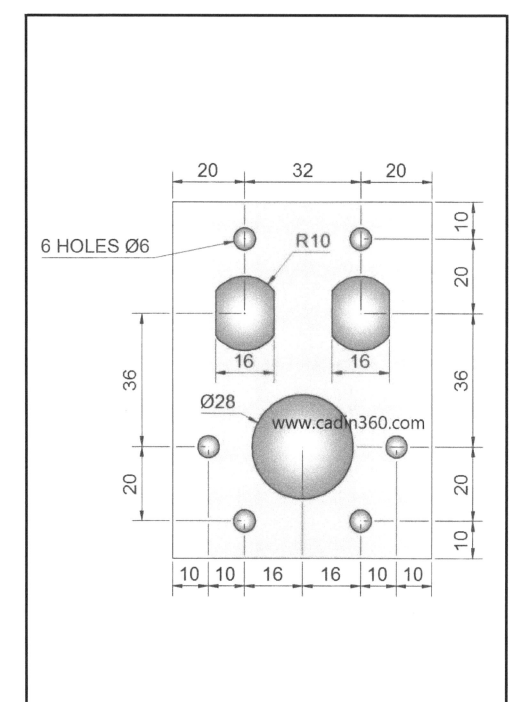

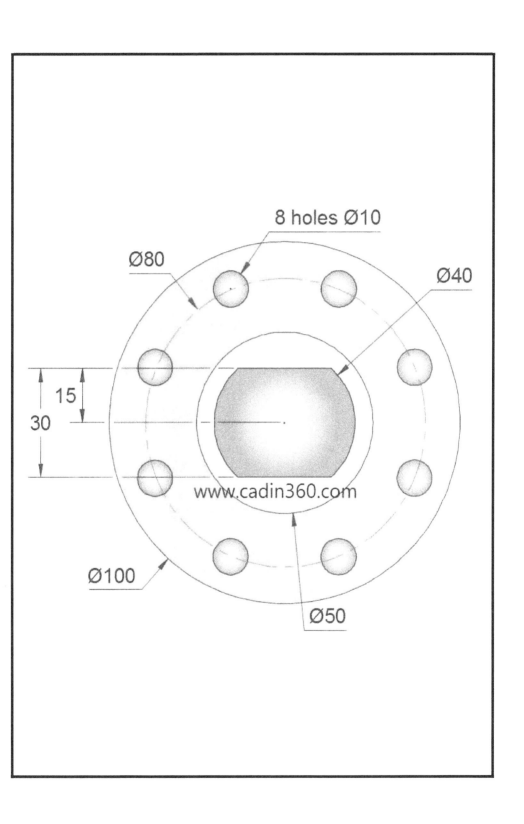

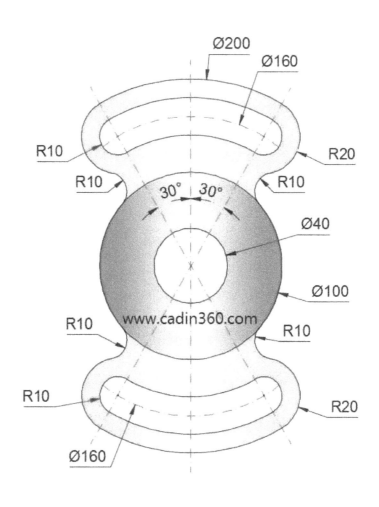

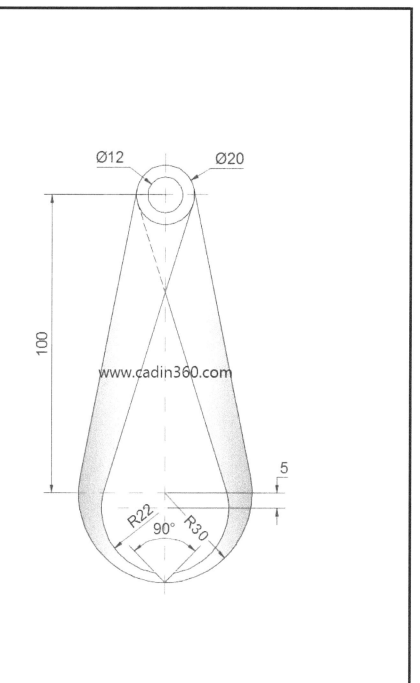

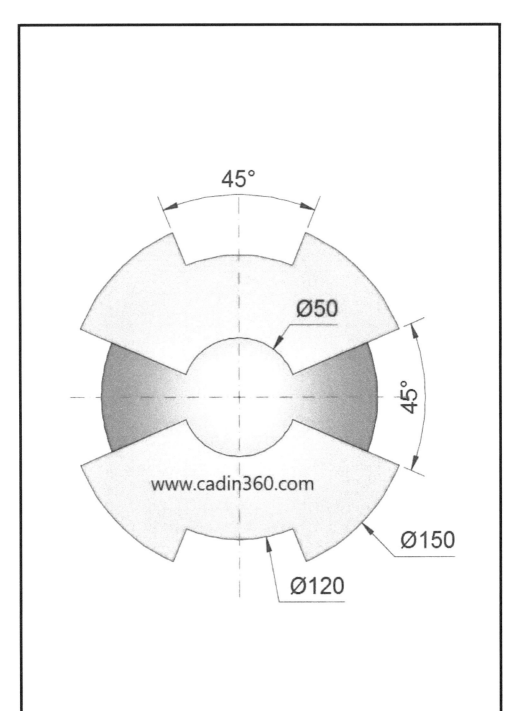

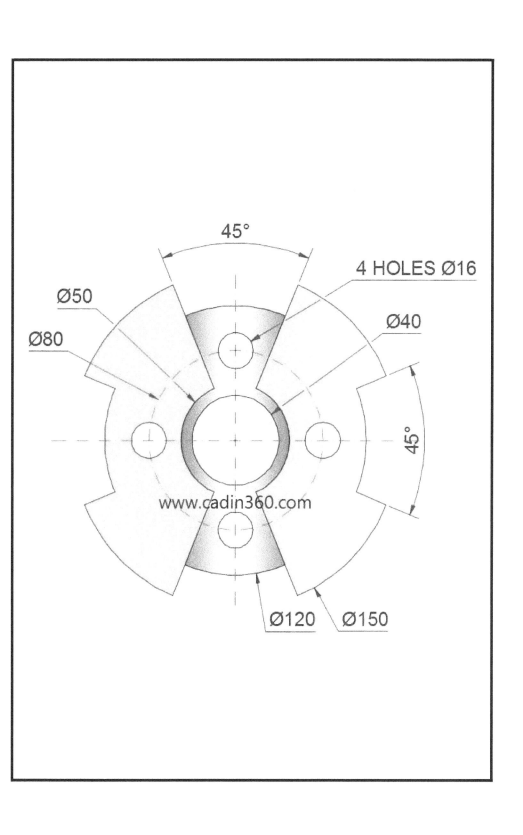

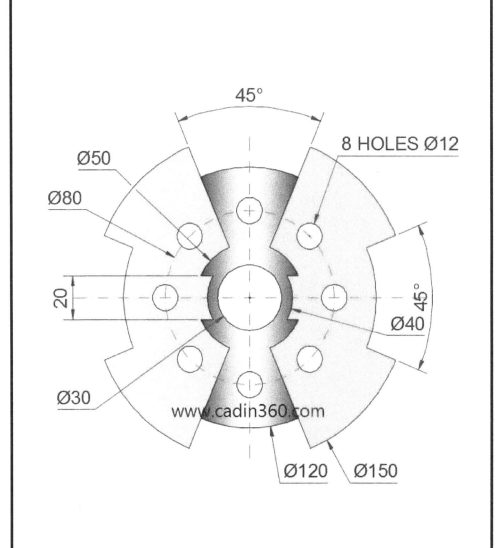

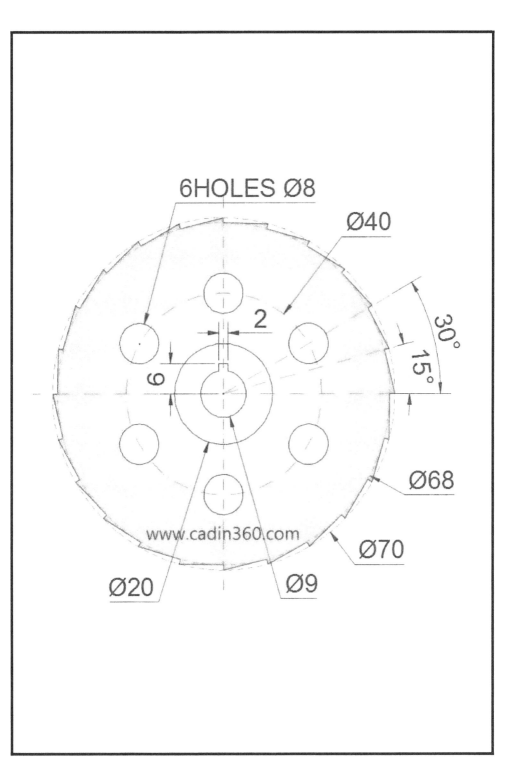

6HOLES Ø8

Ø40

30°

15°

2

9

Ø68

www.cadin360.com

Ø70

Ø20

Ø9

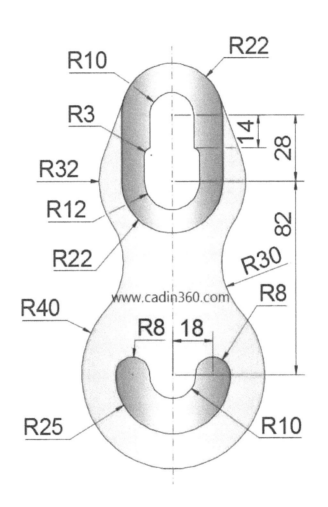

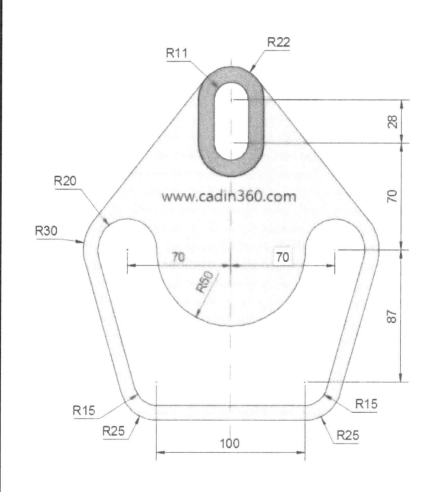

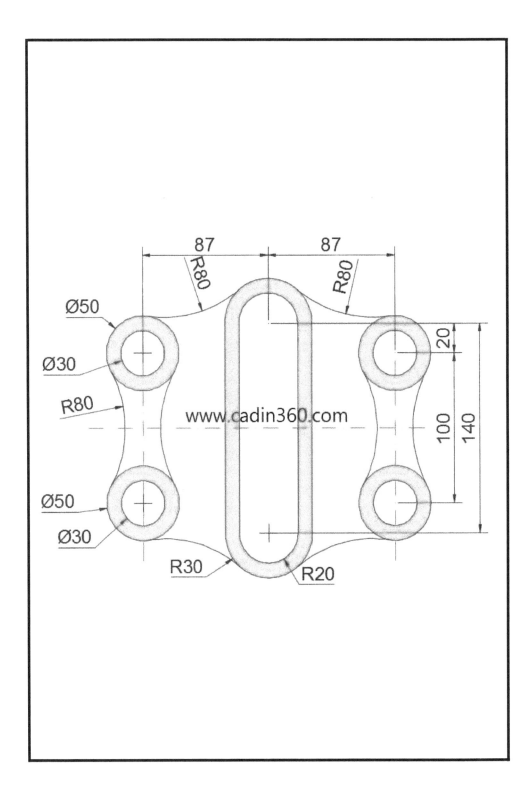

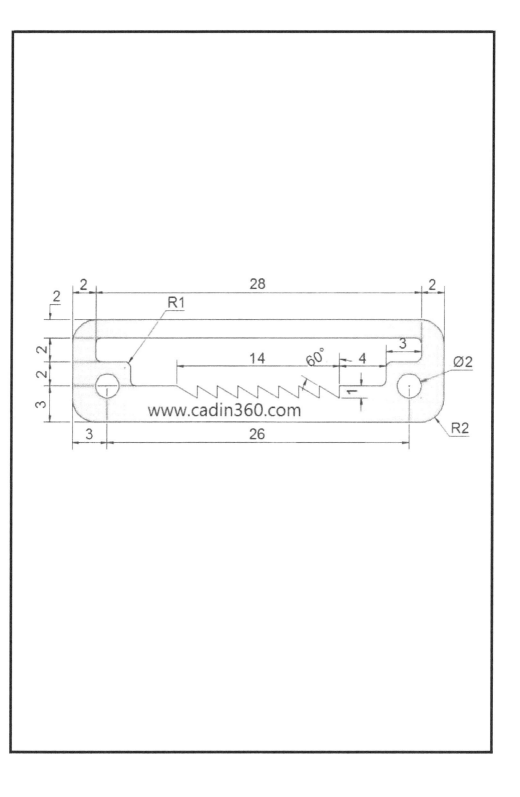

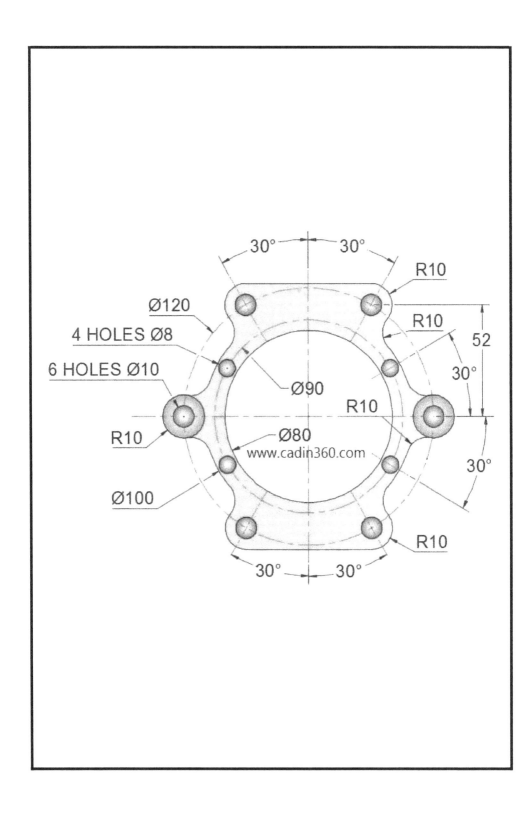

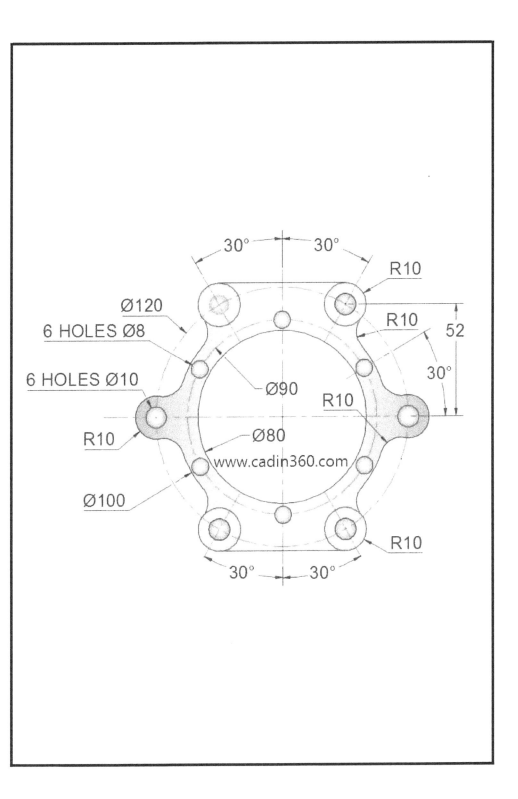

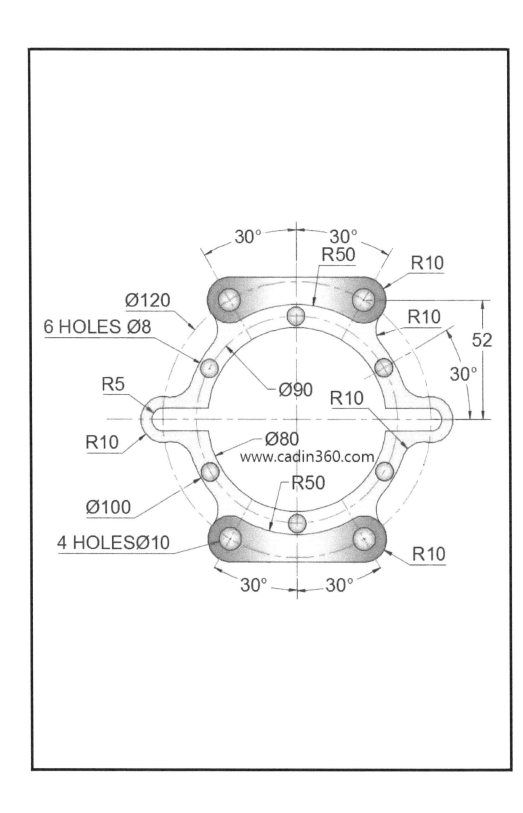

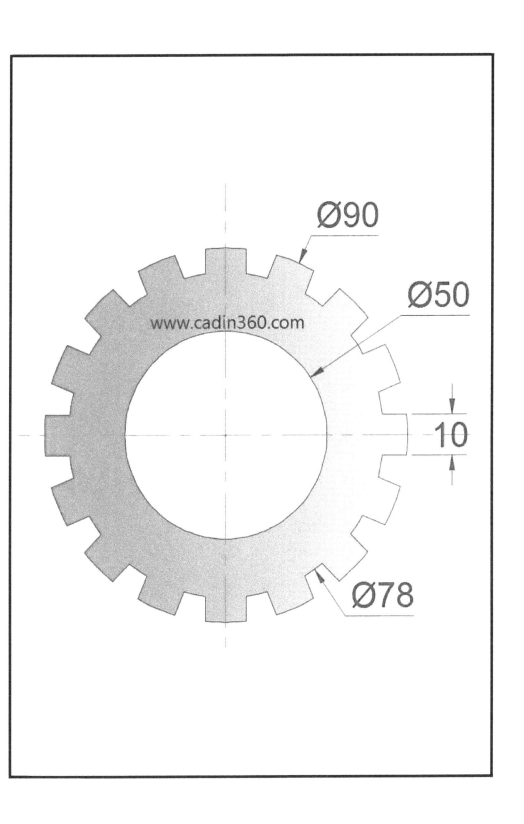

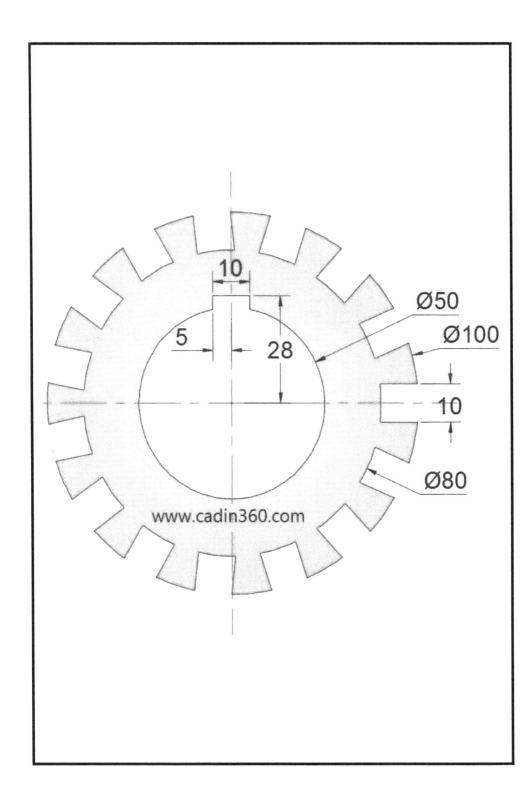

www.cadin360.com

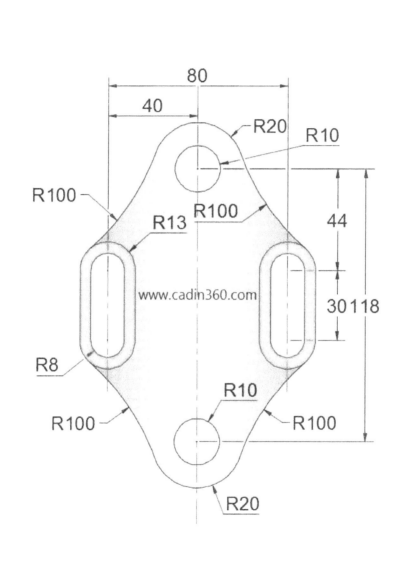

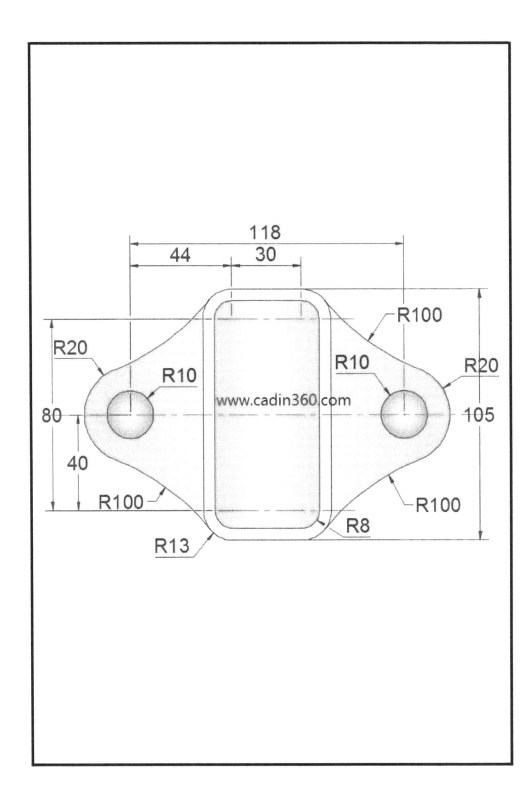

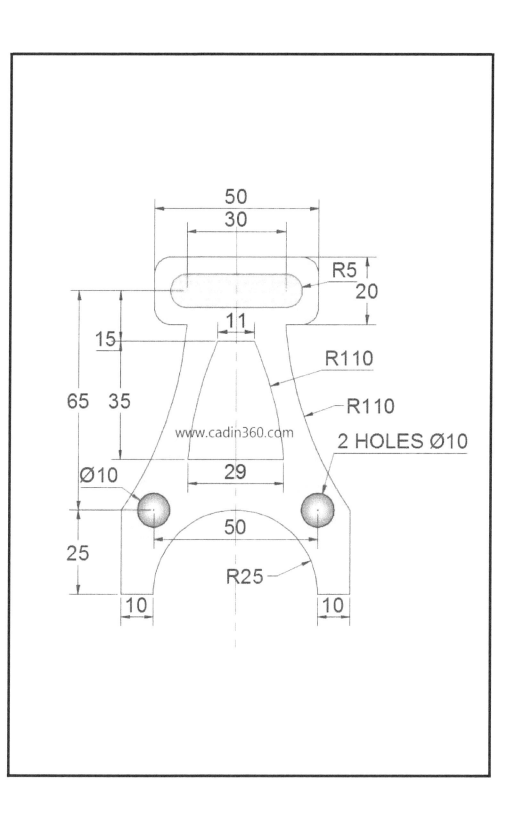

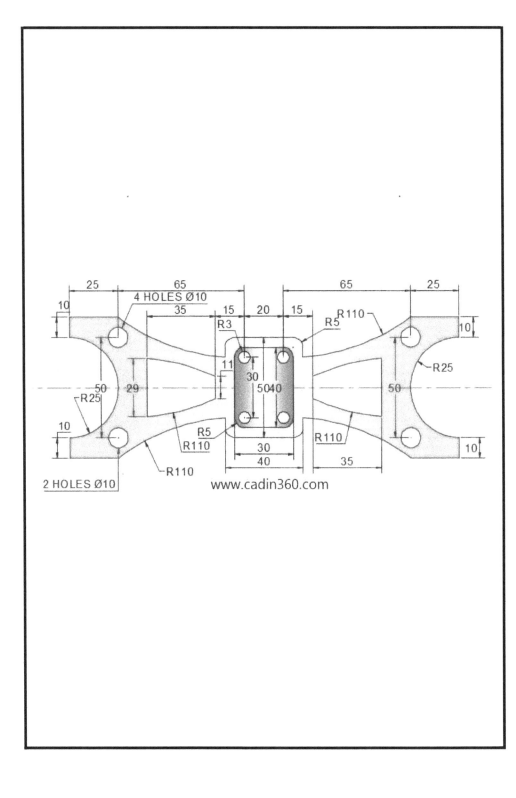

www.cadin360.com

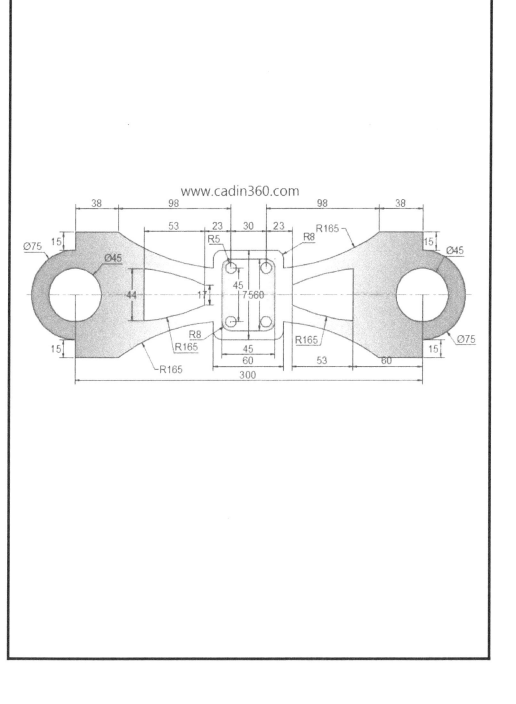
www.cadin360.com

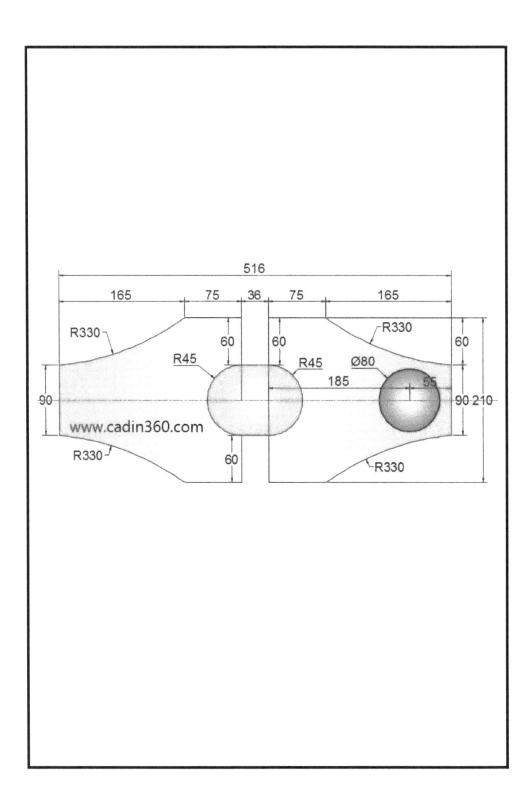

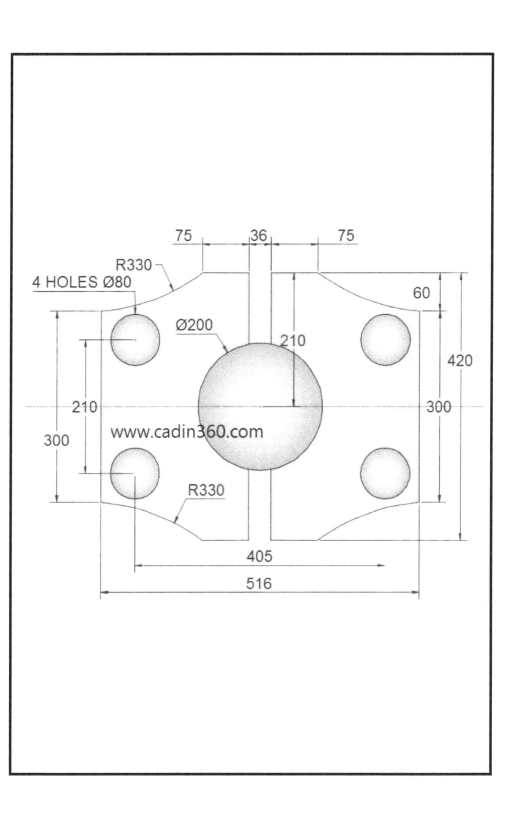

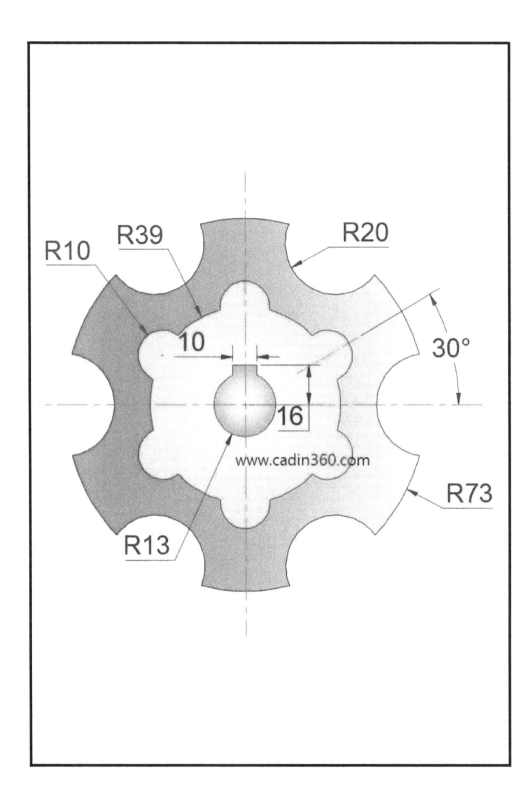

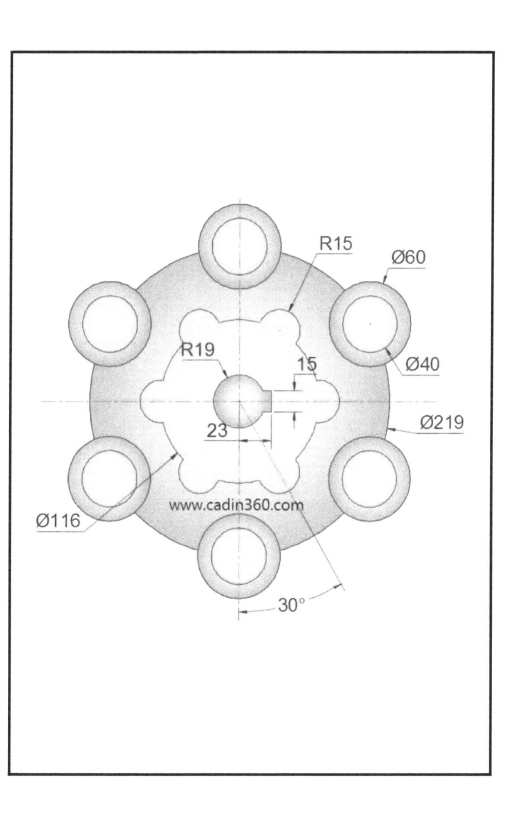

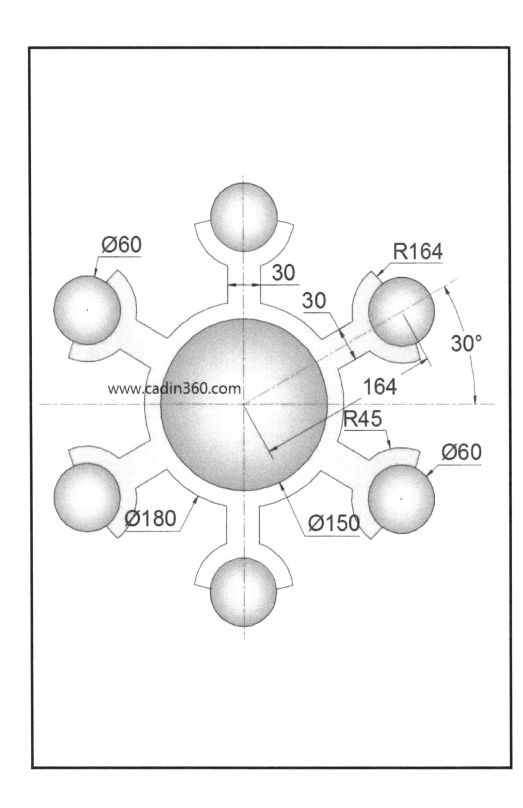

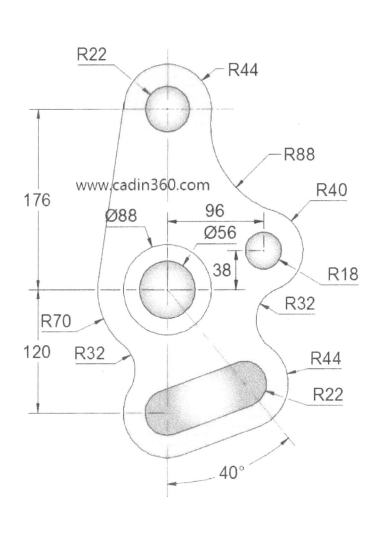

R22 R44

R88

R40

176 www.cadin360.com

Ø88 96 Ø56 R18

38

R70 R32

120 R32 R44

R22

40°

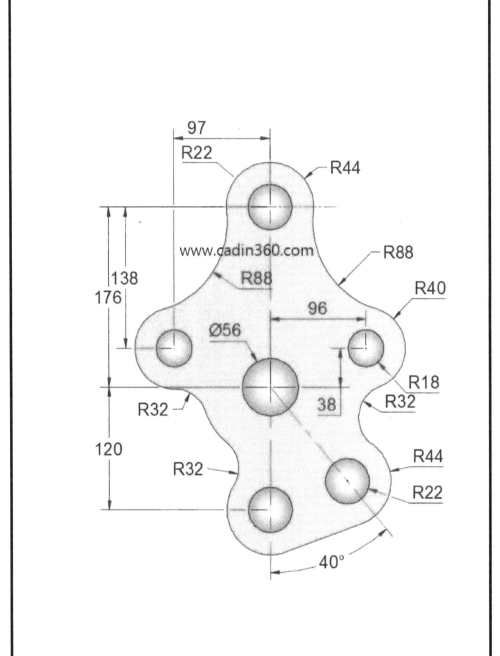

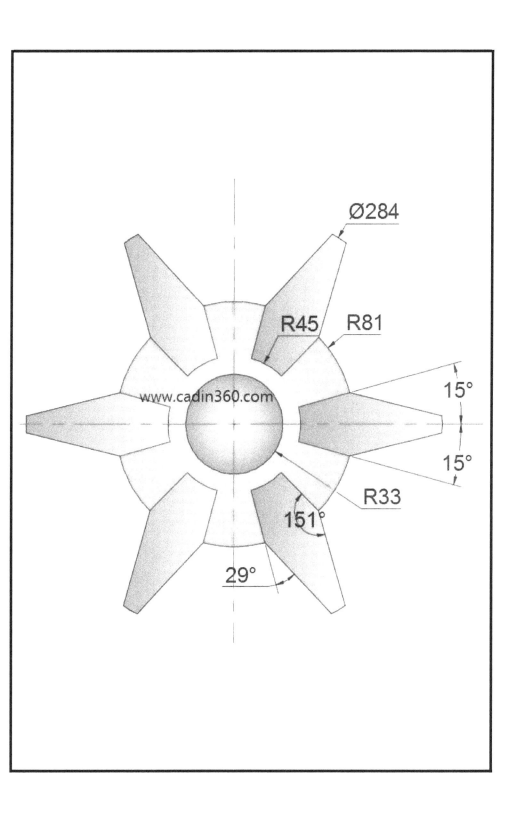

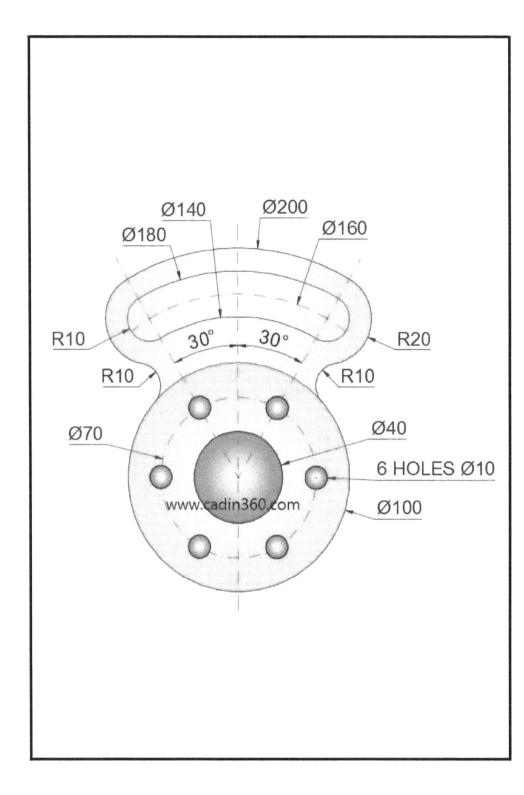

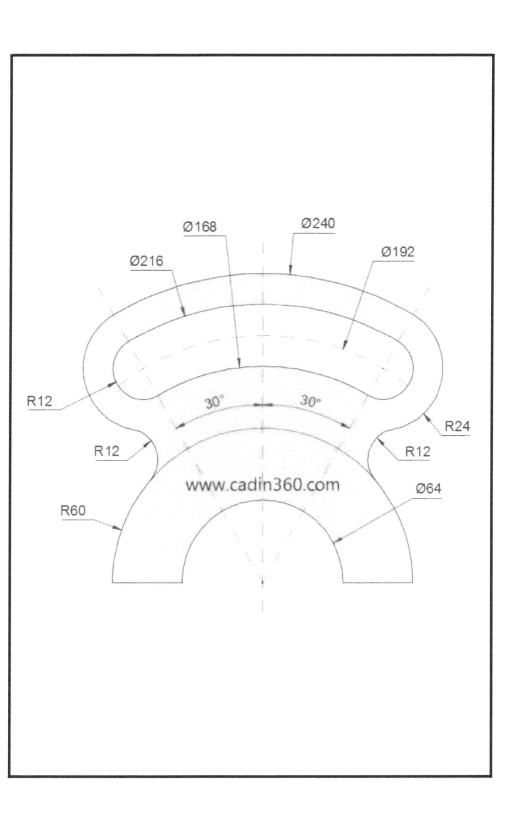

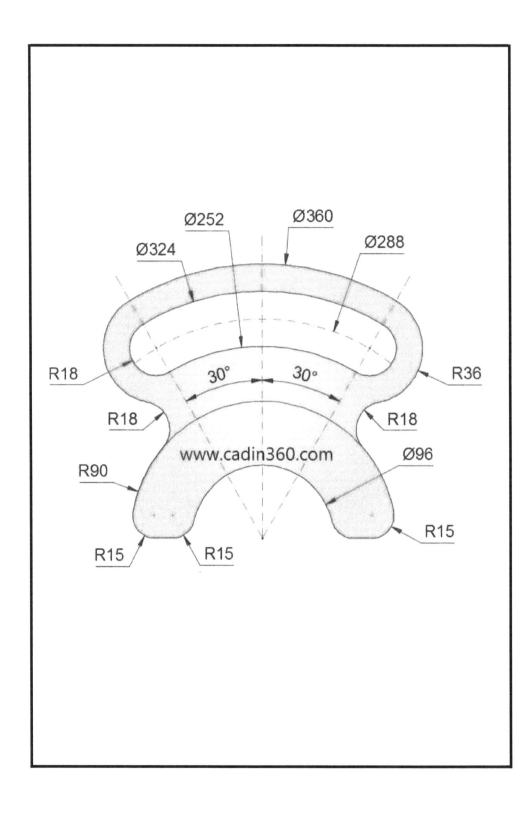

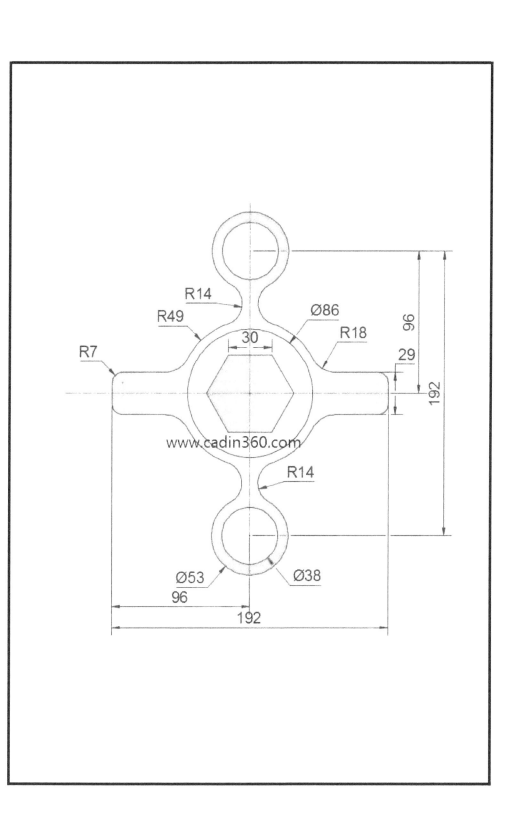

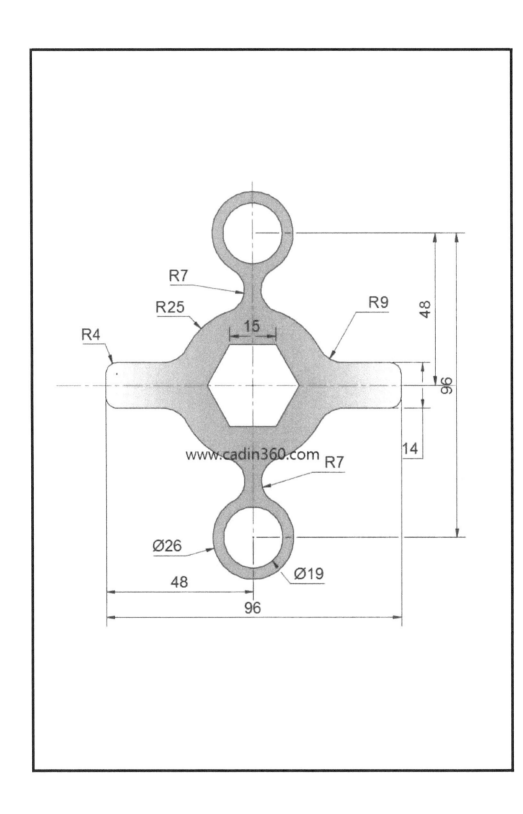

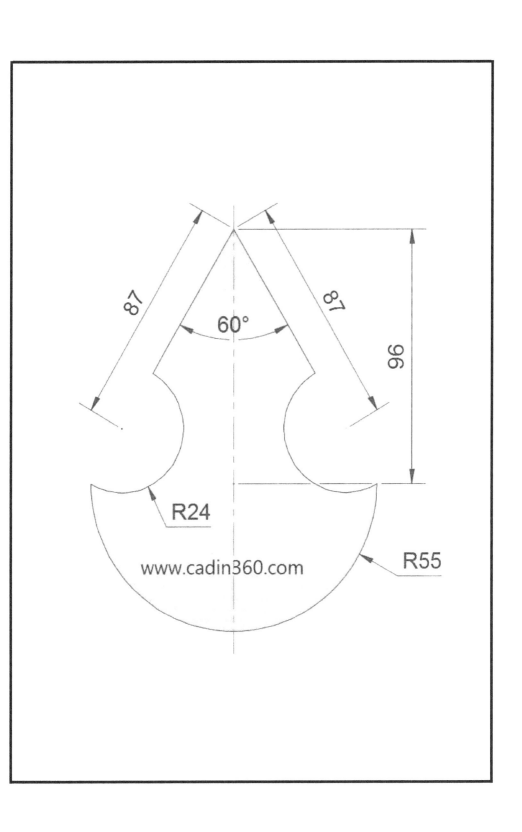

87

87

60°

96

R24

R55

www.cadin360.com

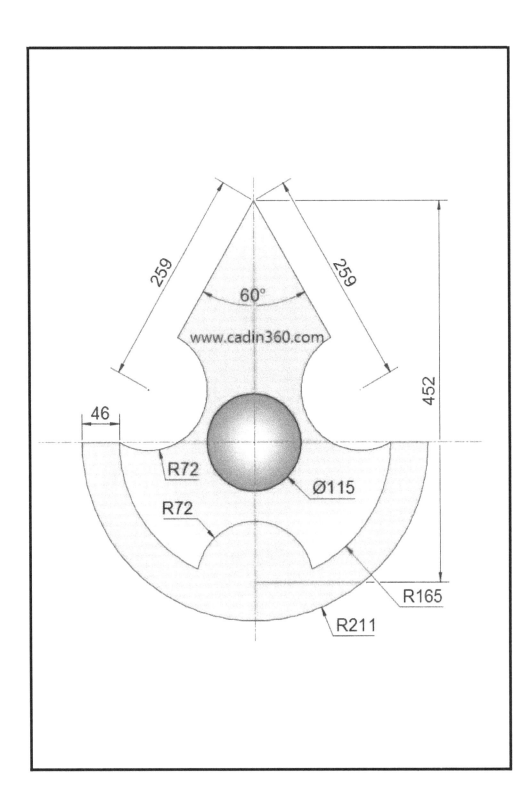

www.cadin360.com

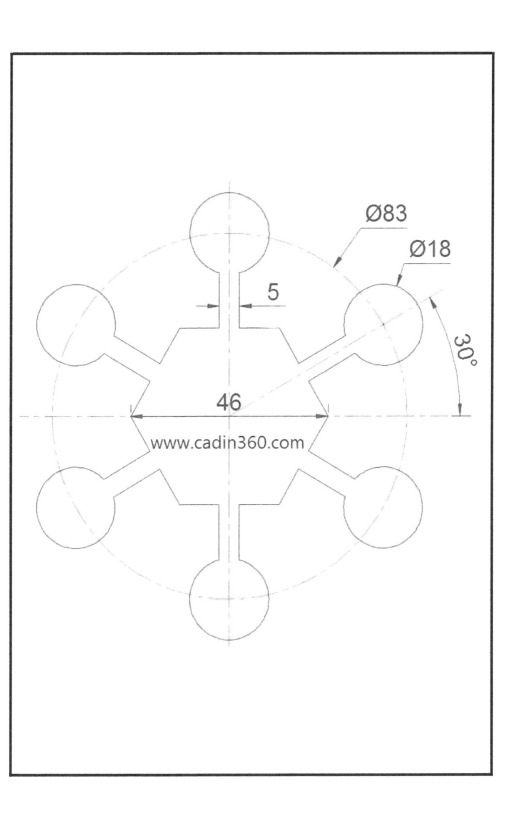

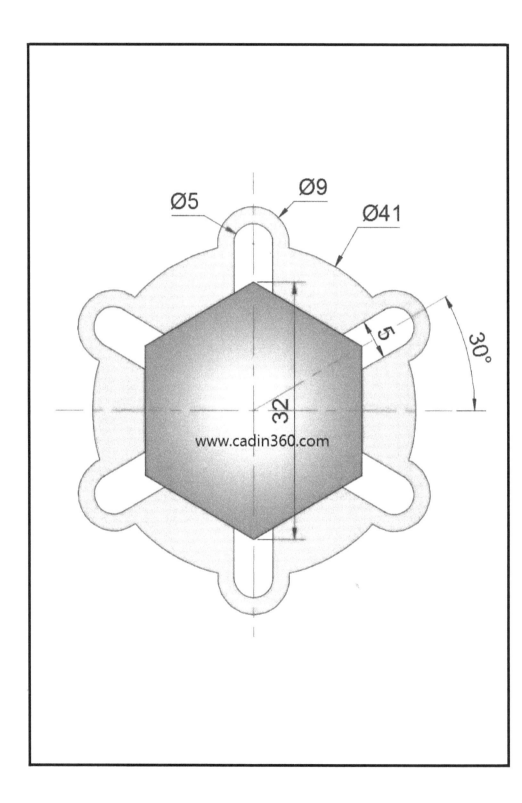

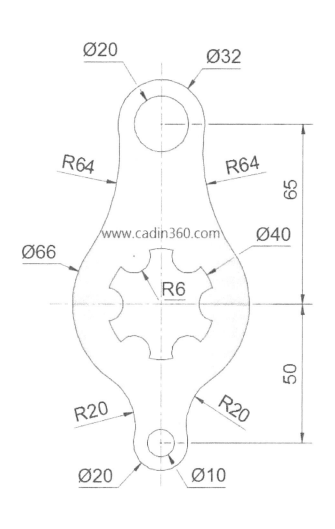

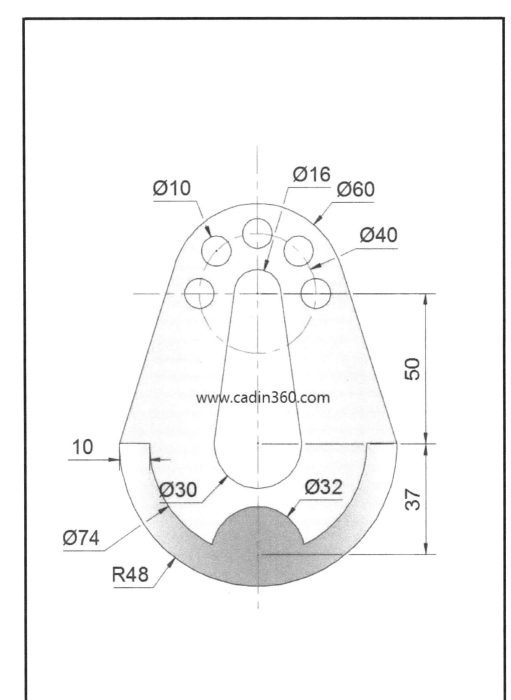

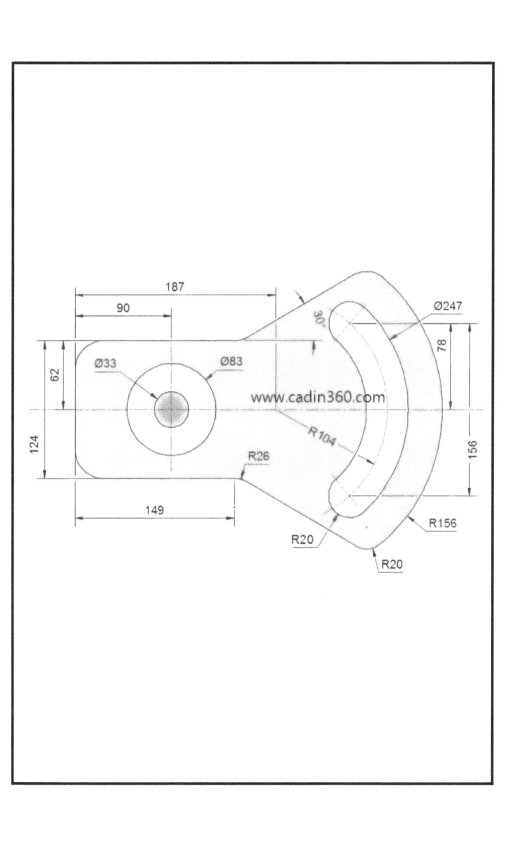

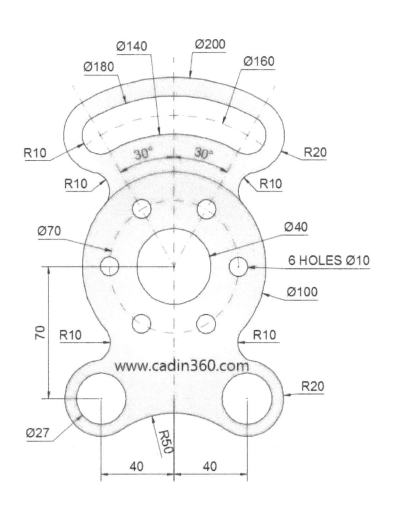

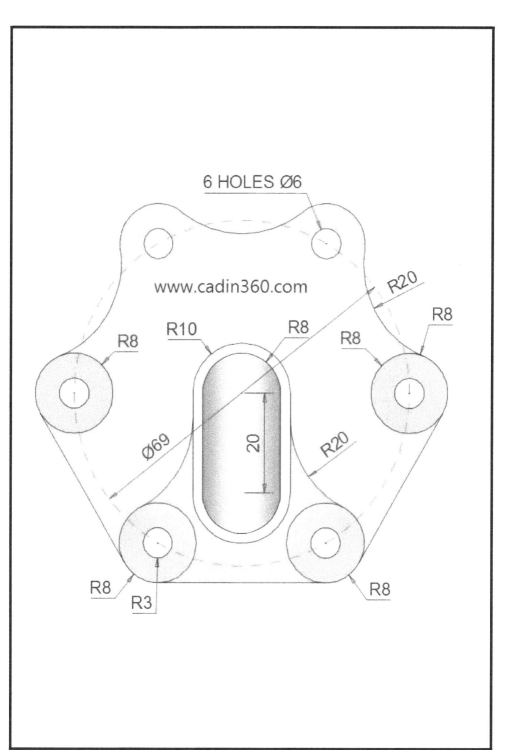

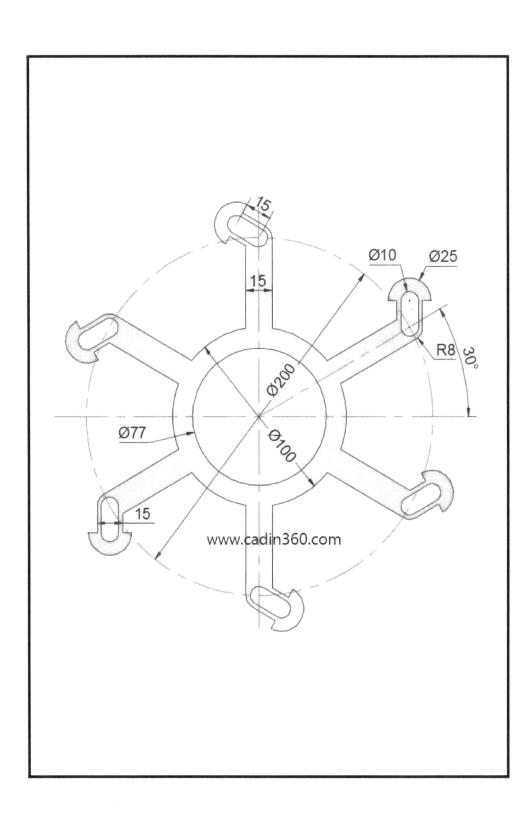

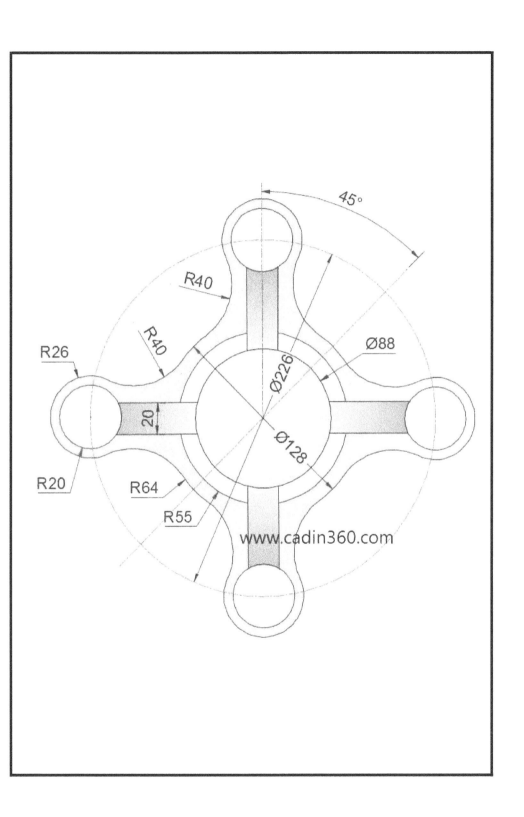

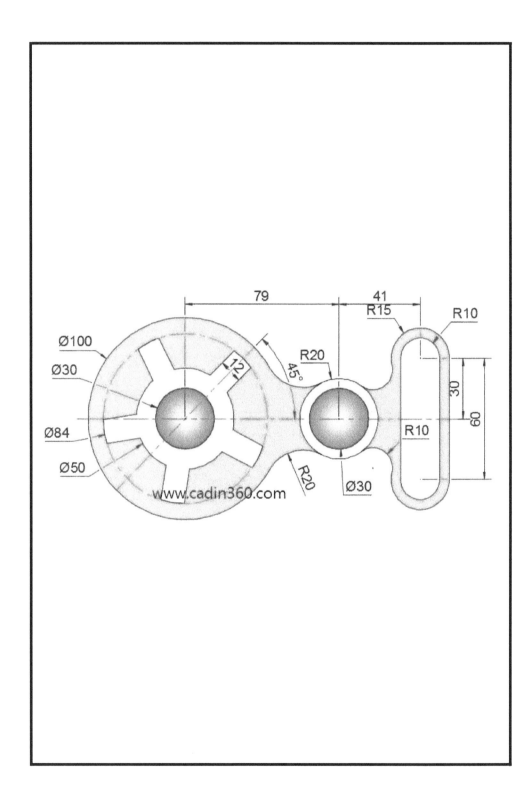

www.cadin360.com

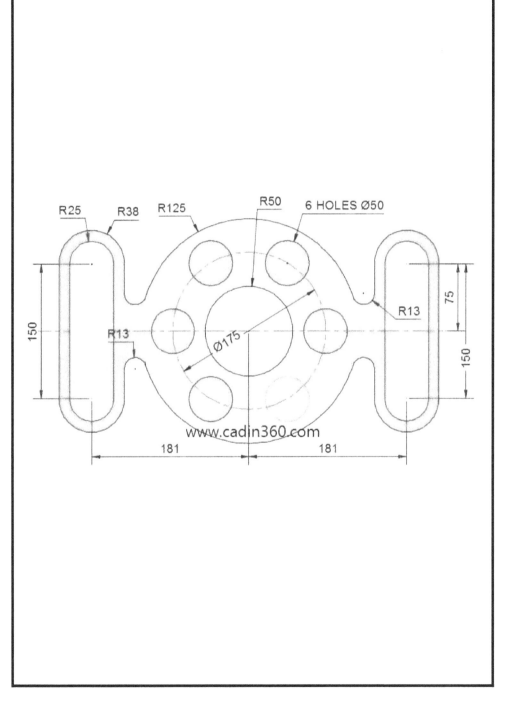

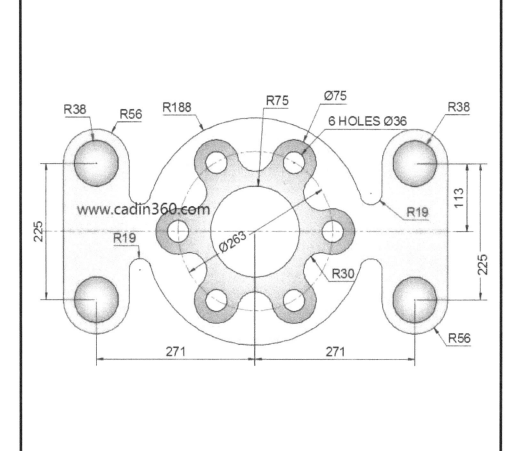

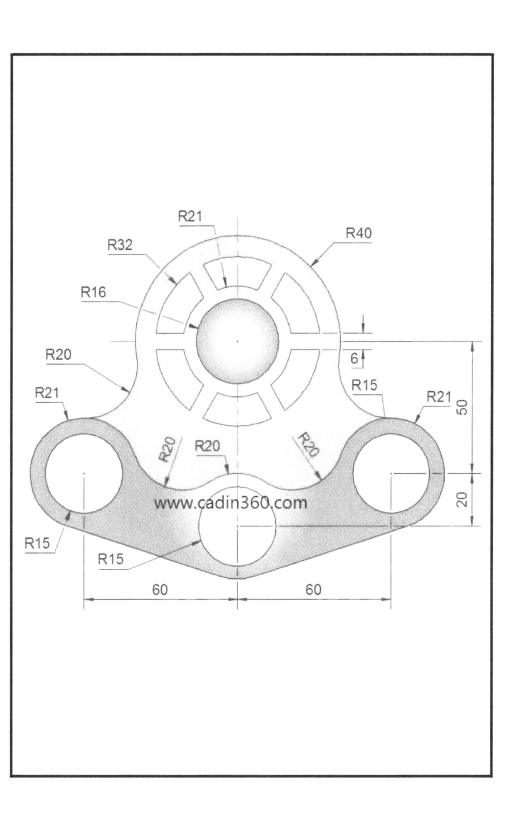

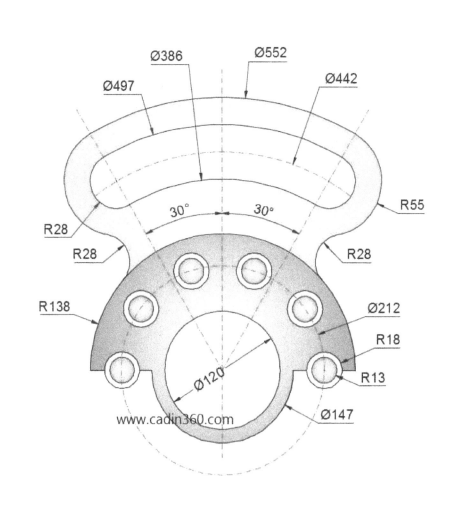

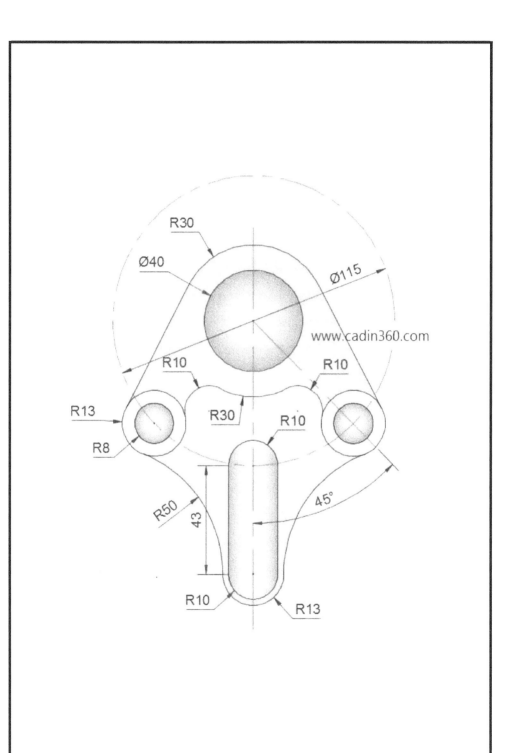

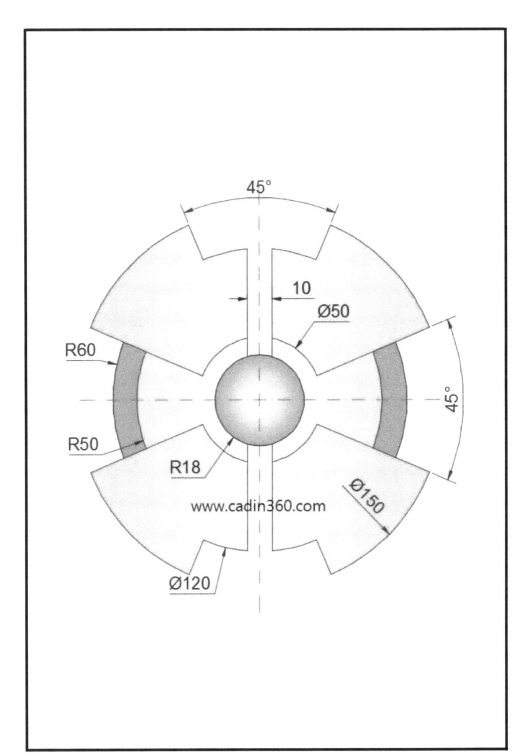
www.cadin360.com

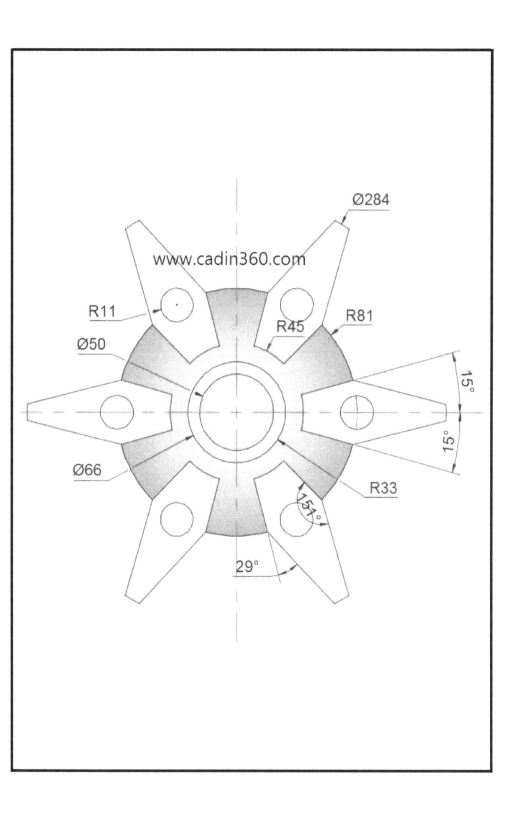

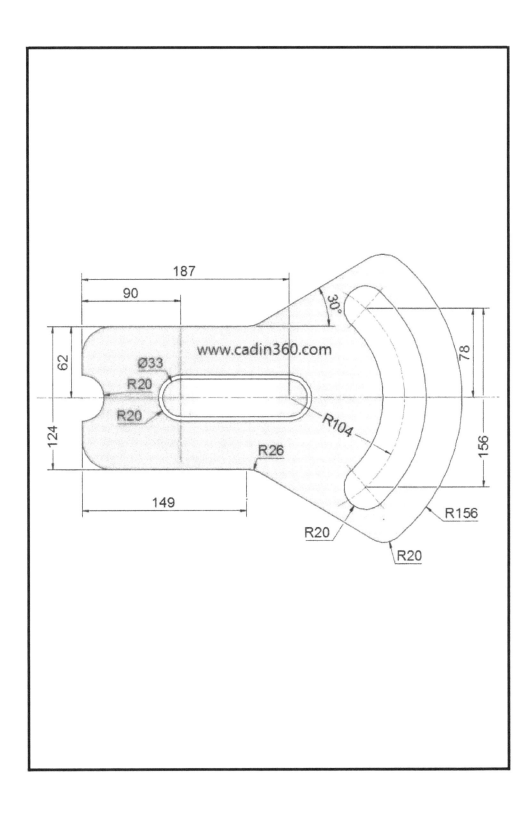

www.cadin360.com

3D EXERCISES

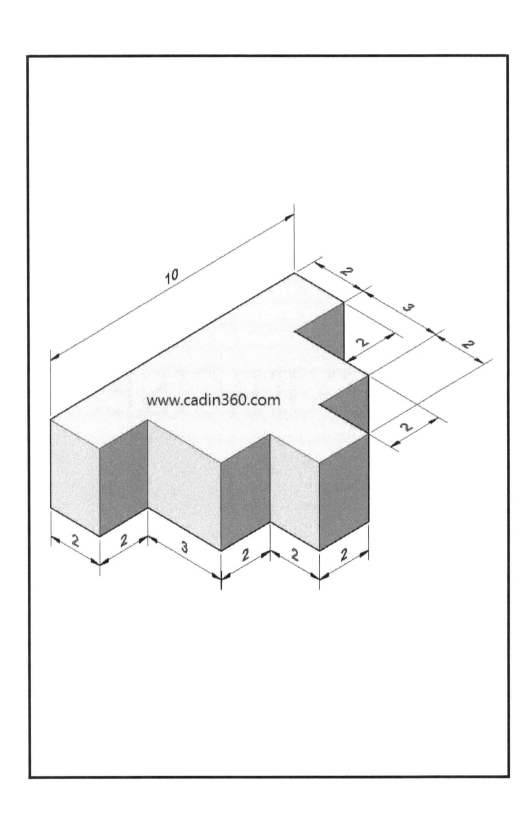

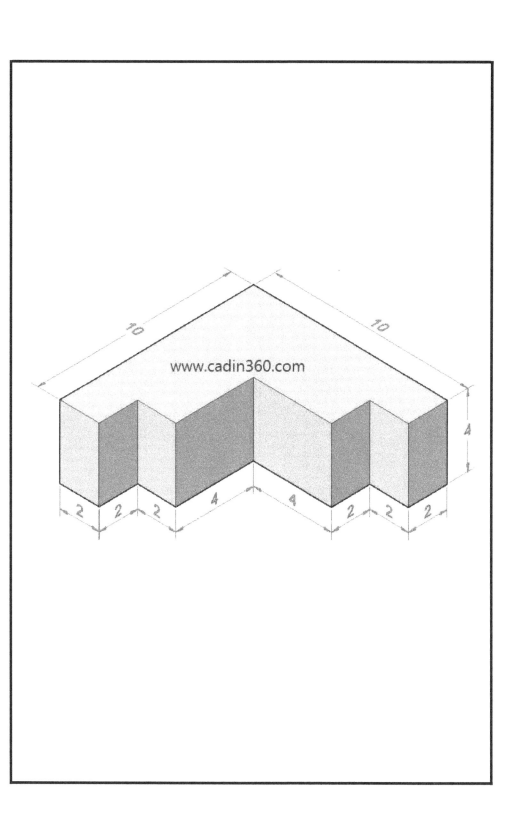

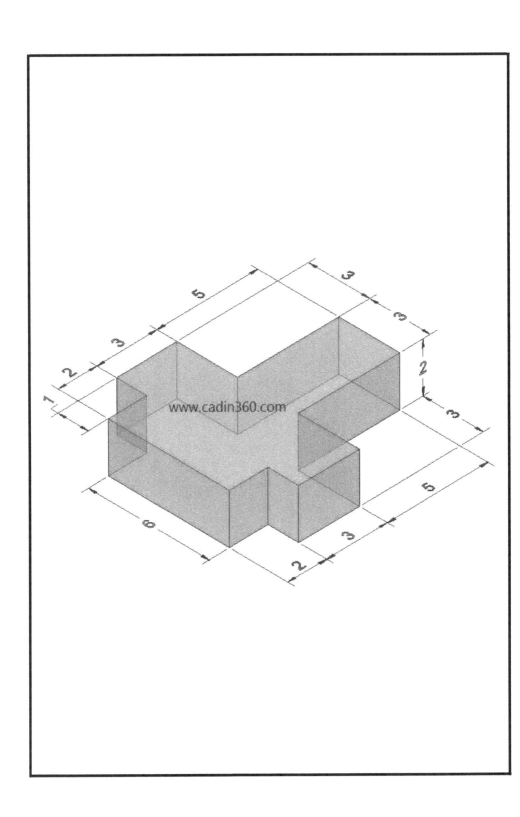

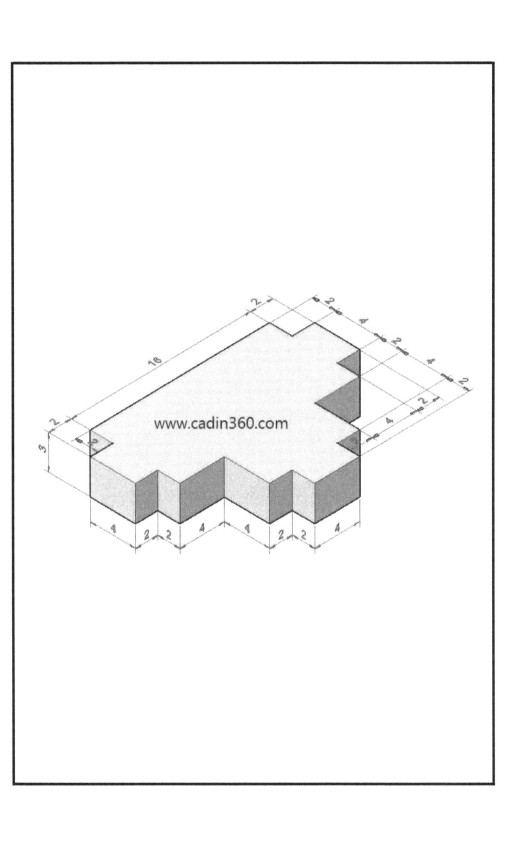

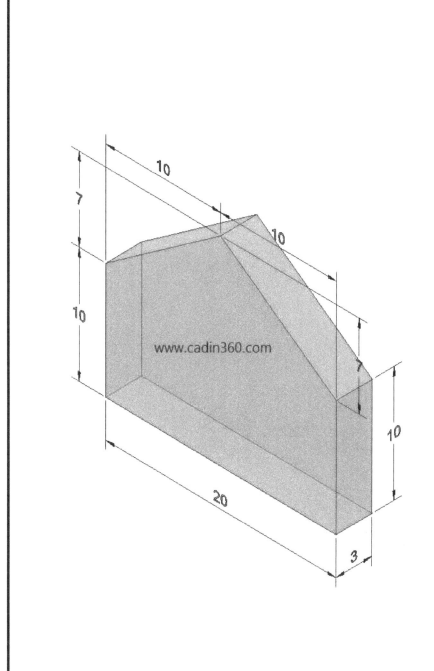

www.cadin360.com

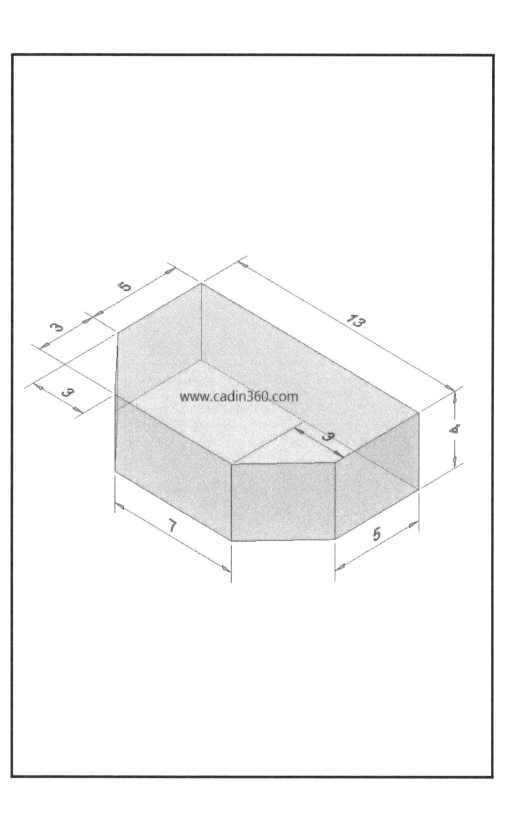

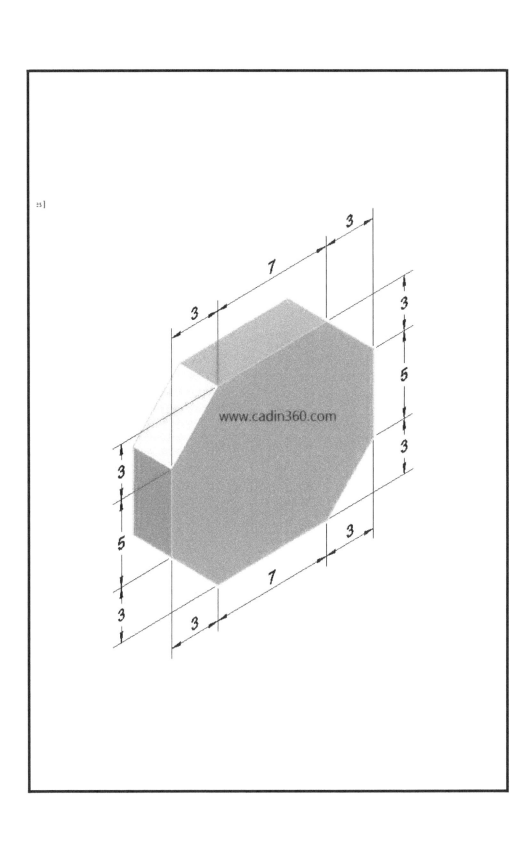

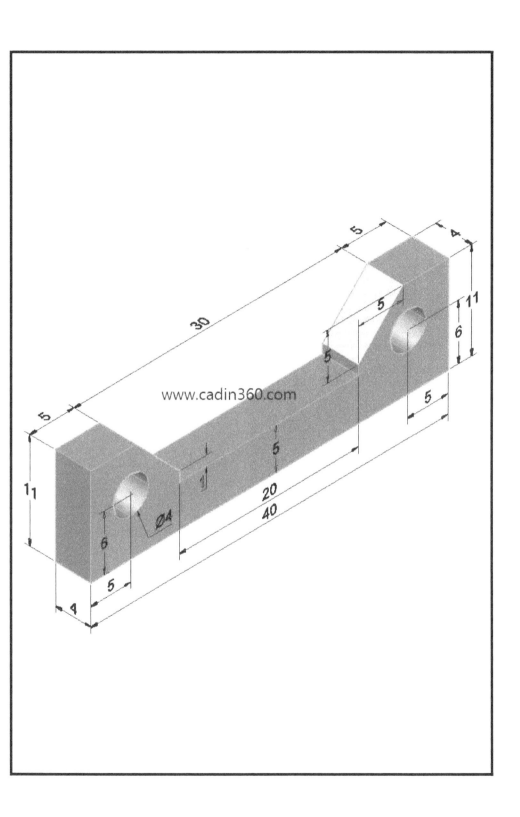

www.cadin360.com

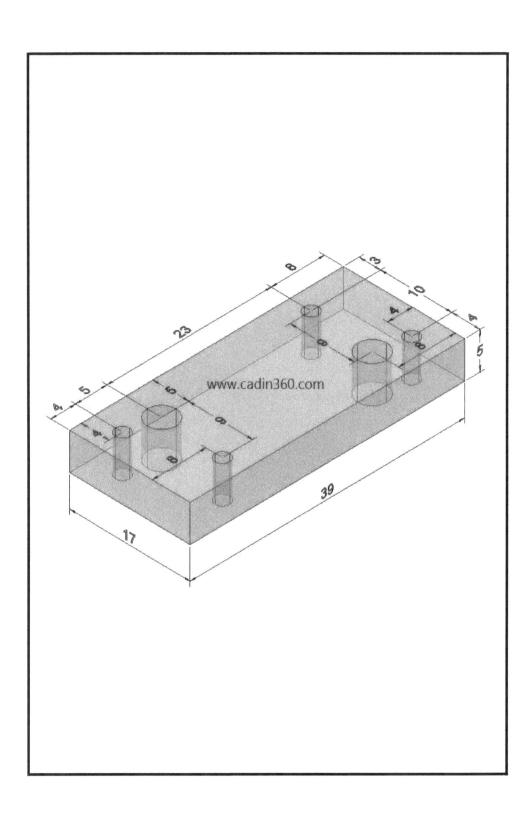

www.cadin360.com

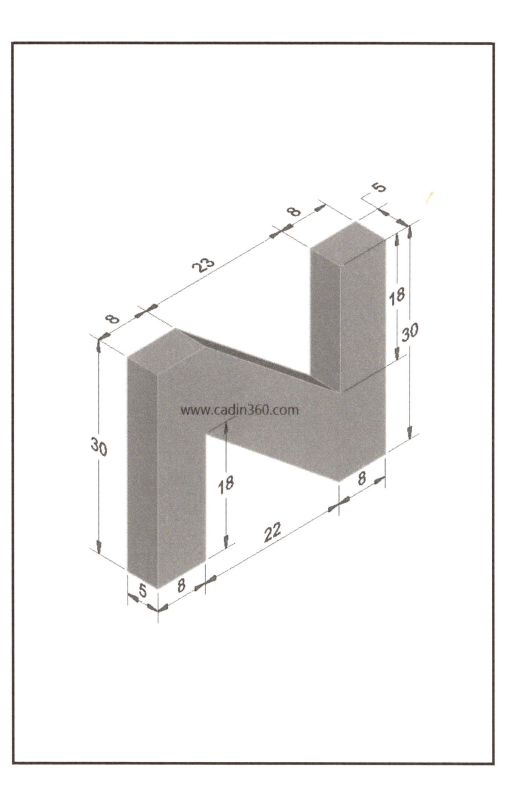

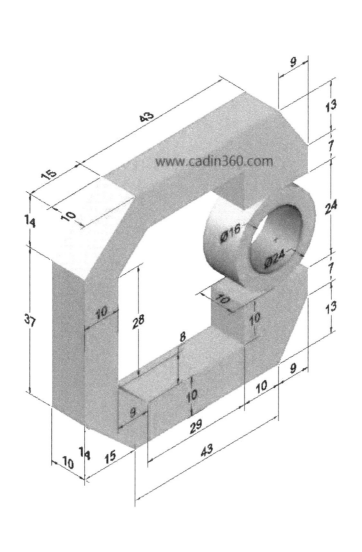

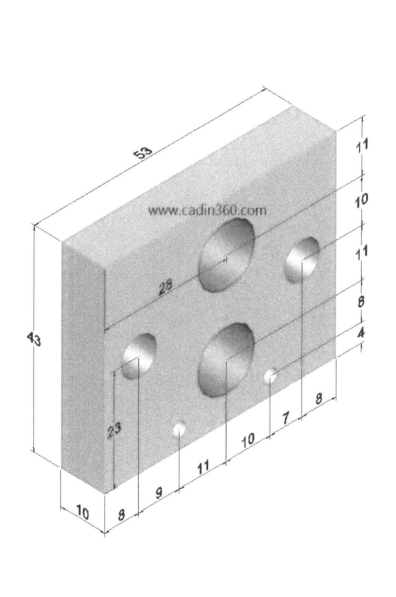

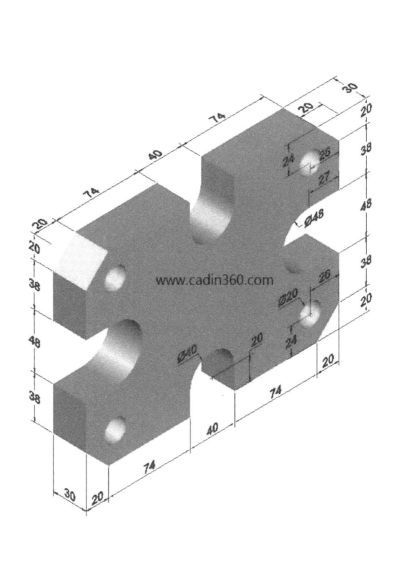

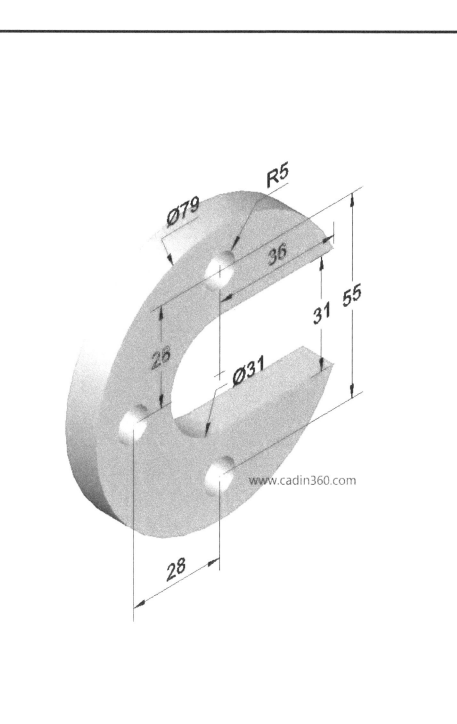

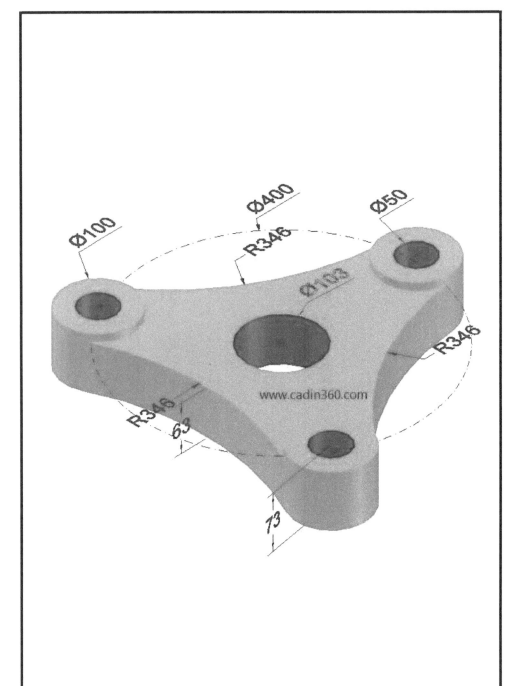

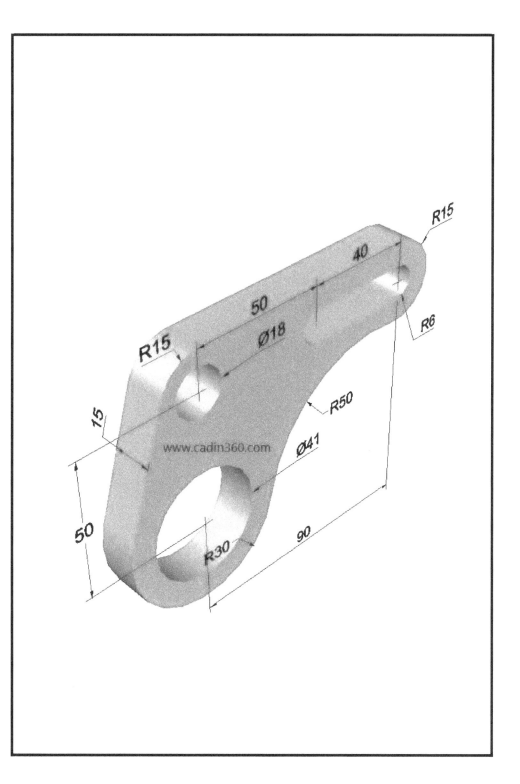

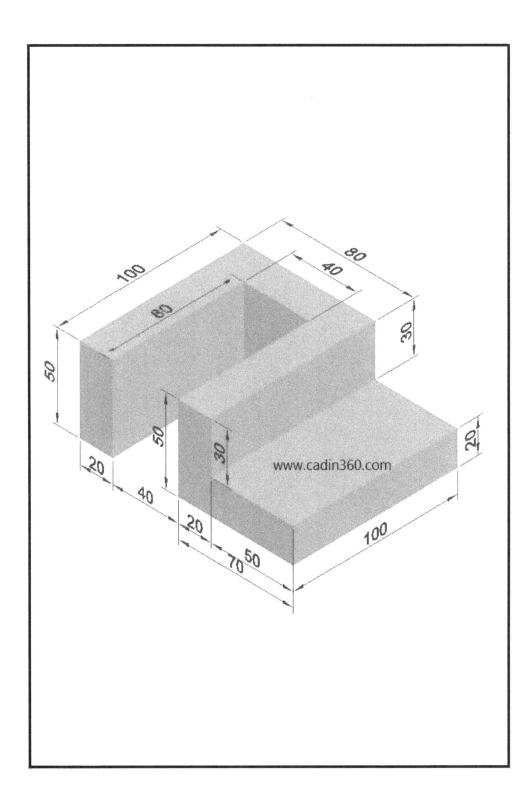

www.cadin360.com

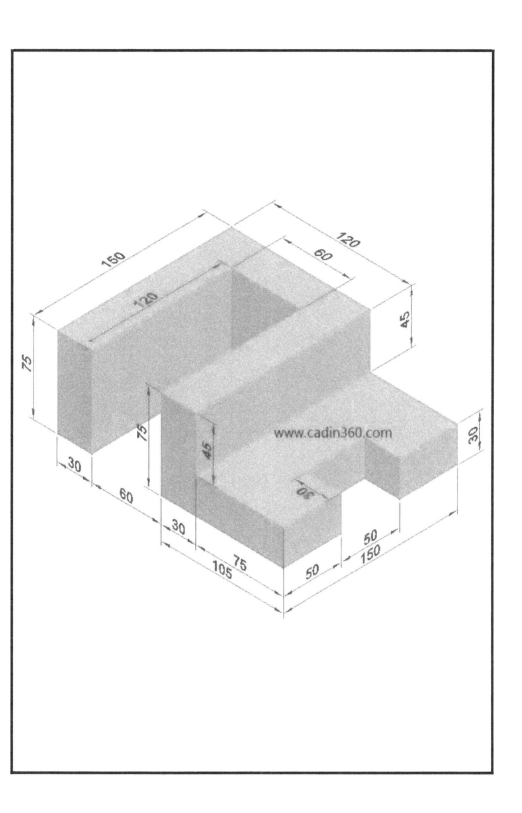

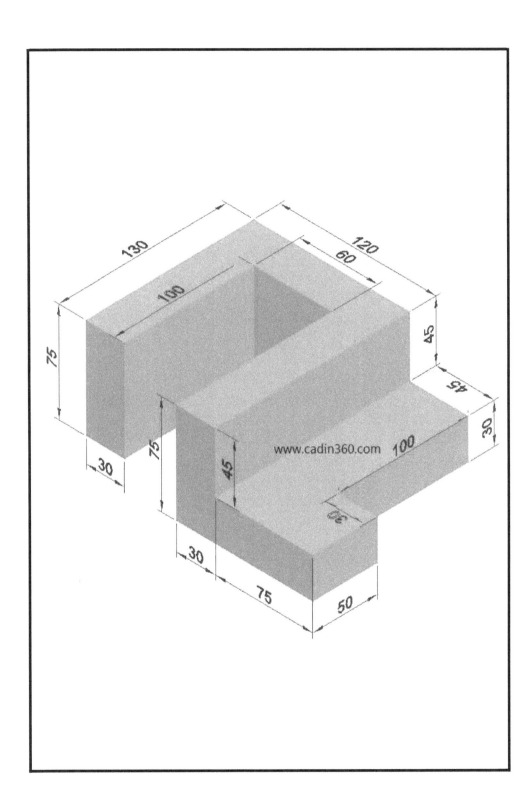

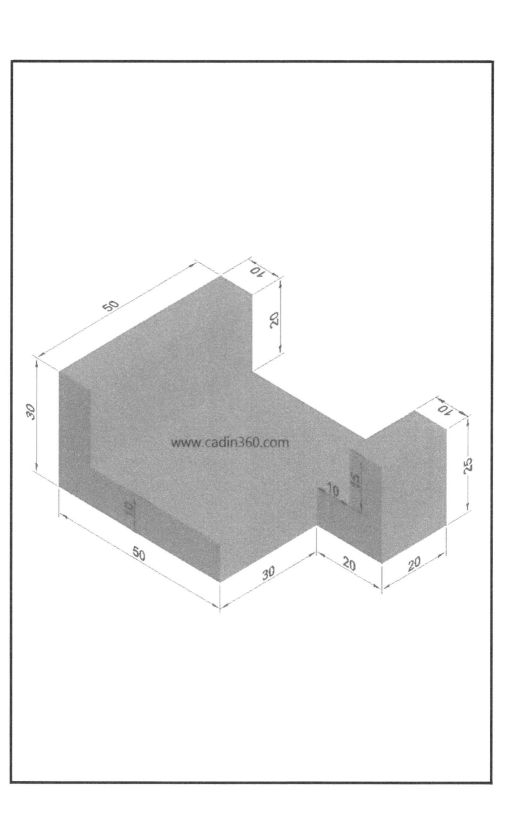

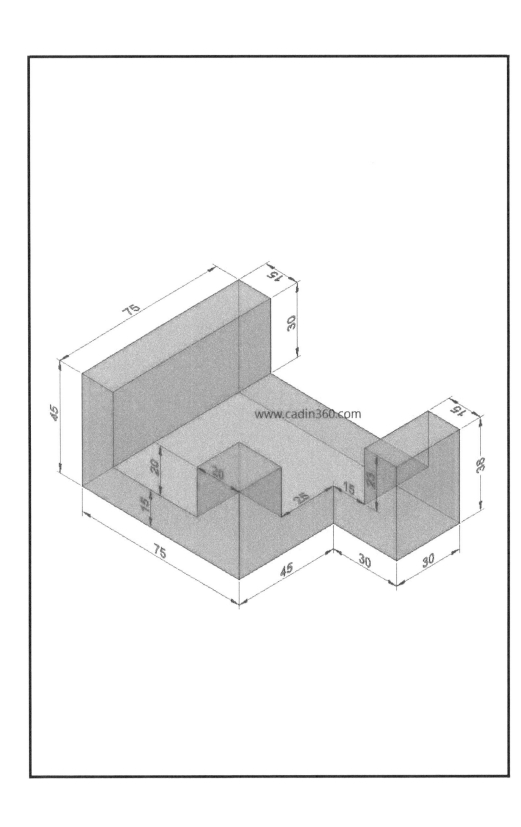

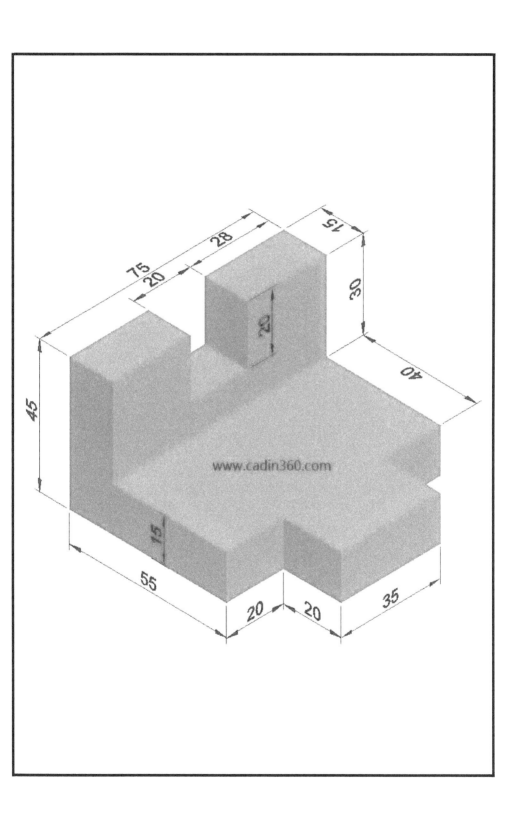

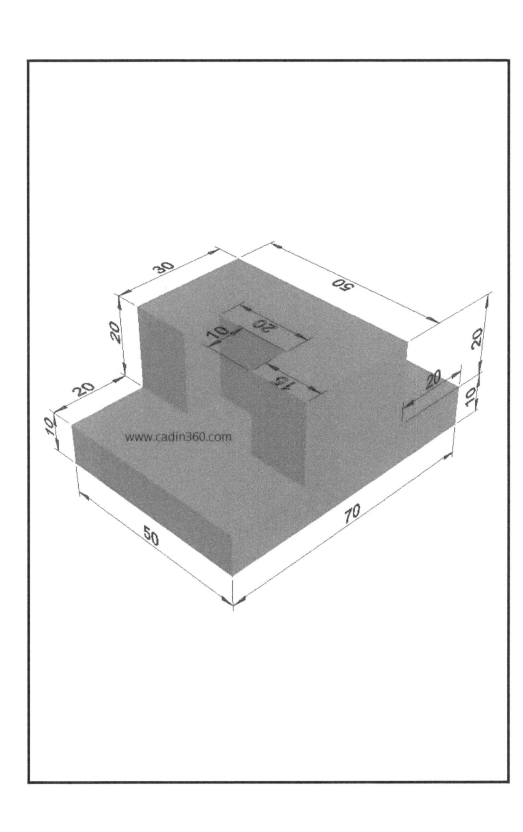

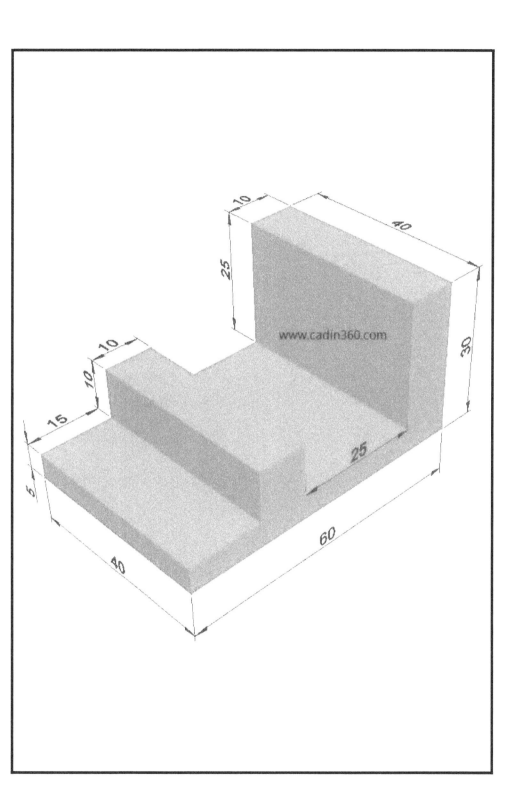

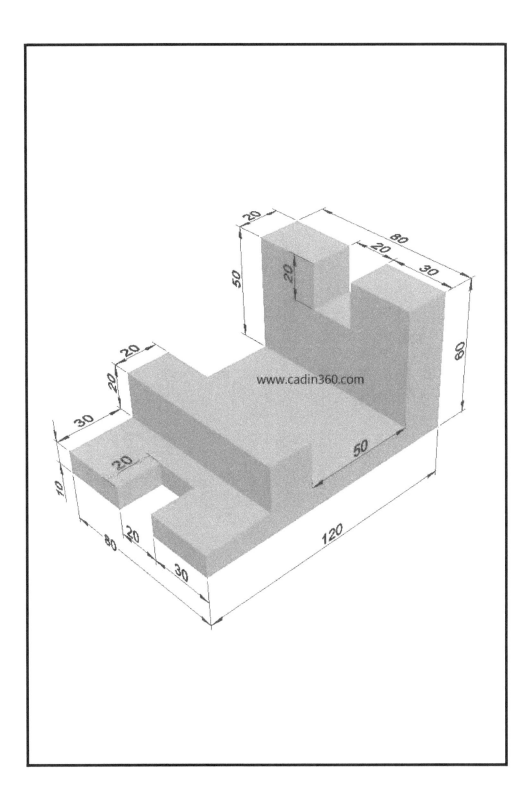

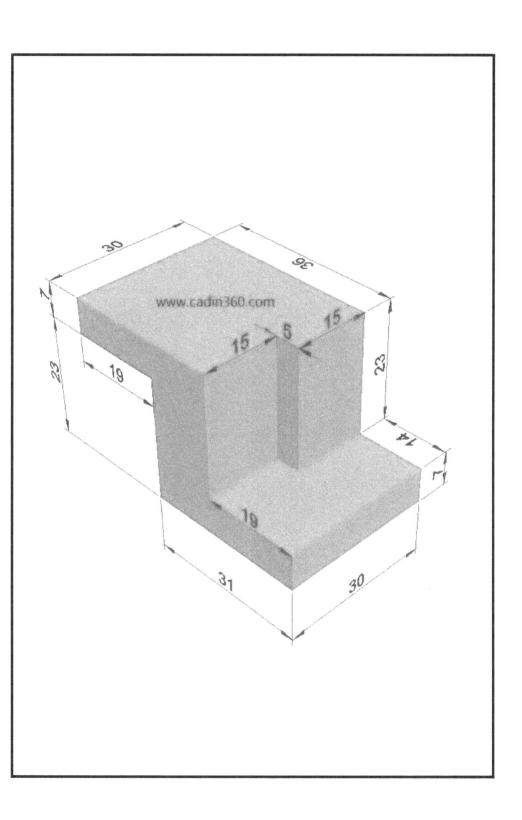
www.cadin360.com

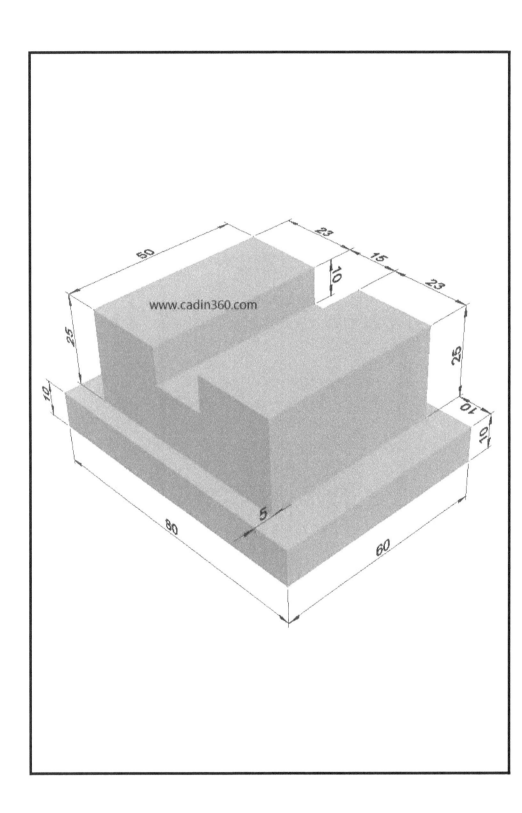

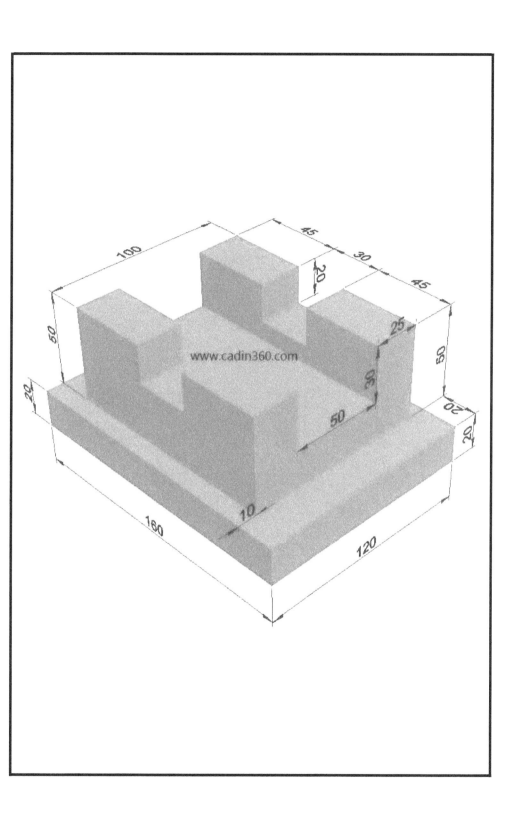

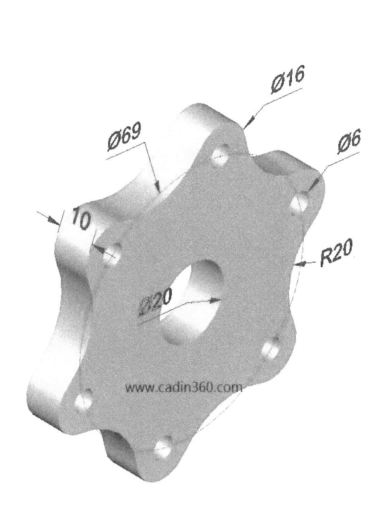

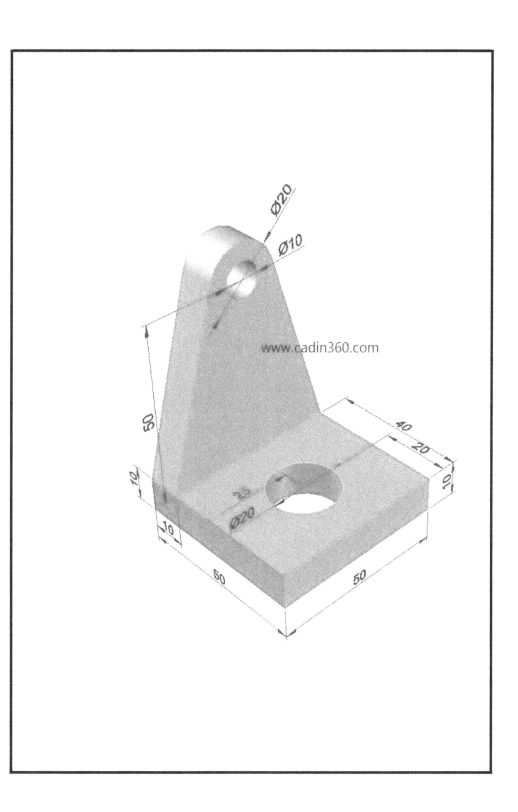

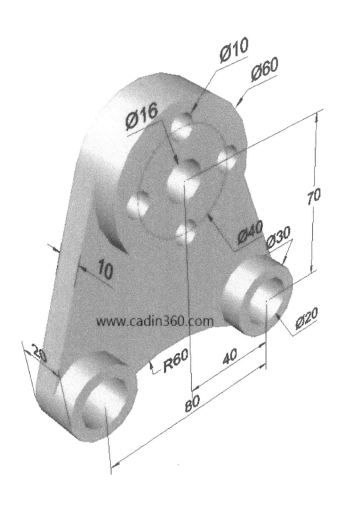

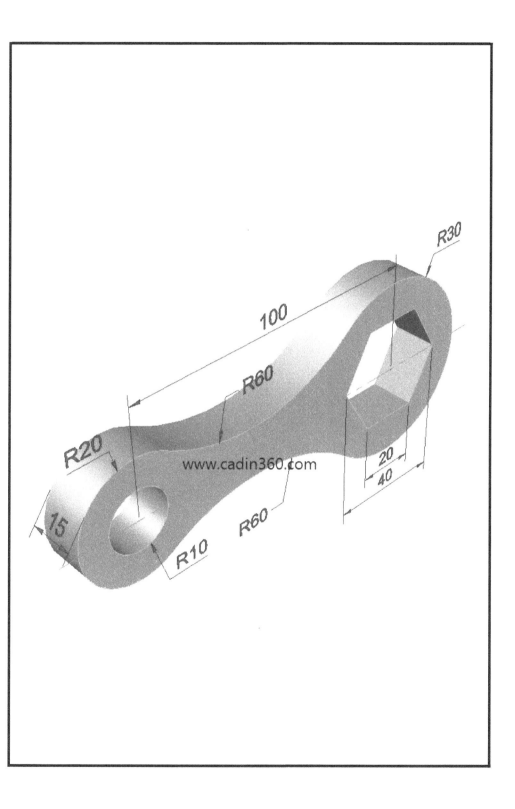

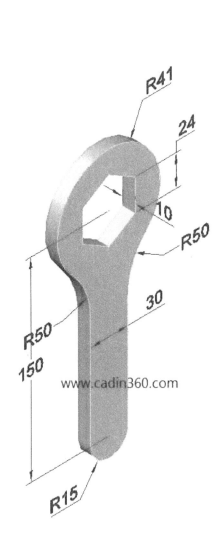

R41

24

10

R50

30

R50

150

www.cadin360.com

R15

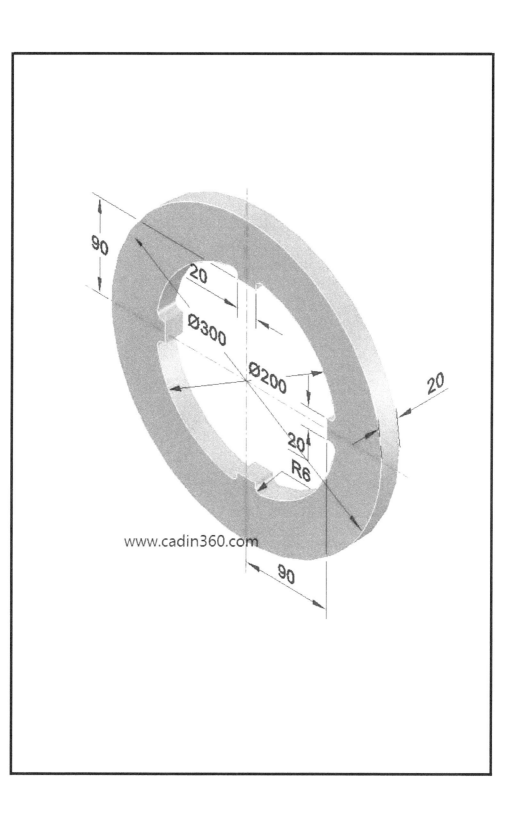

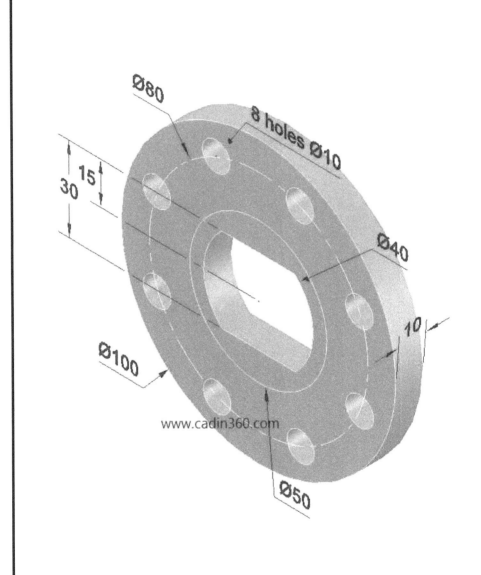

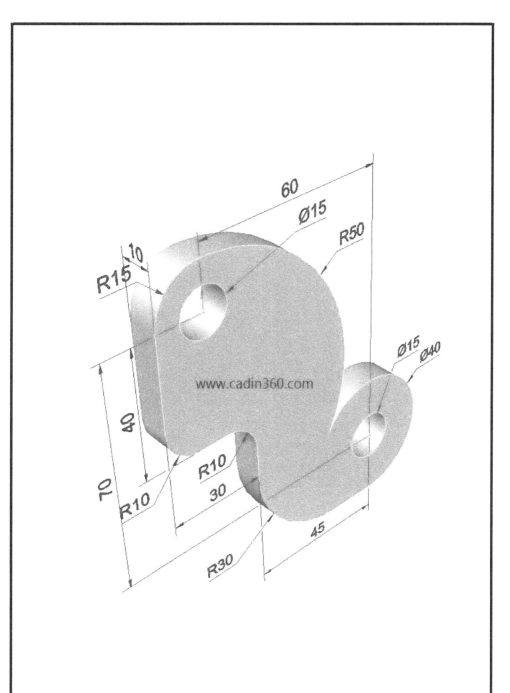

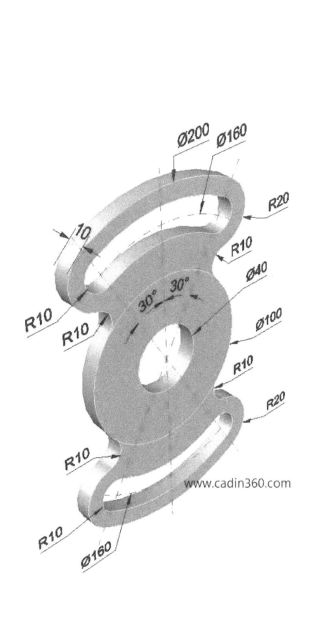

Ø200 Ø160

R20

10

R10

R10 Ø40

R10 Ø100

R10

R10 R20

R10

www.cadin360.com

30° 30°

R10

Ø160

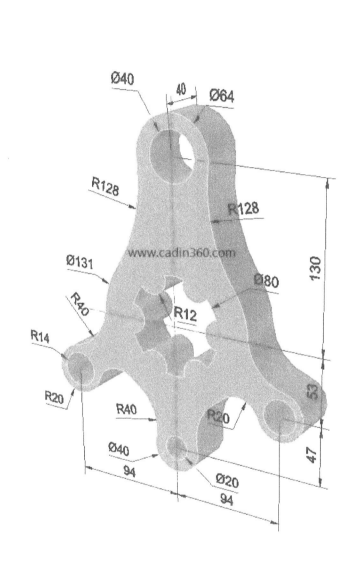

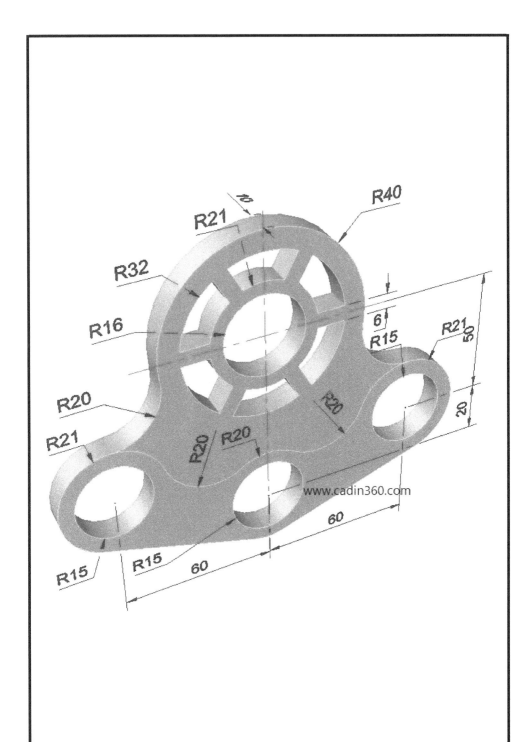

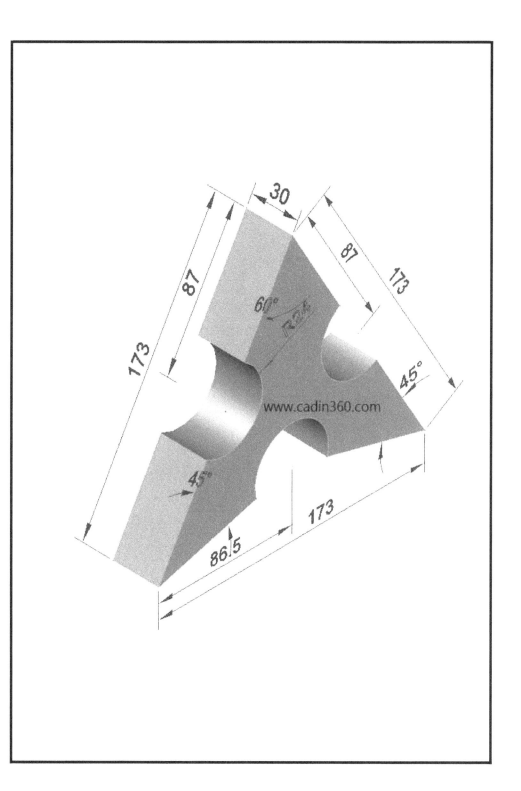

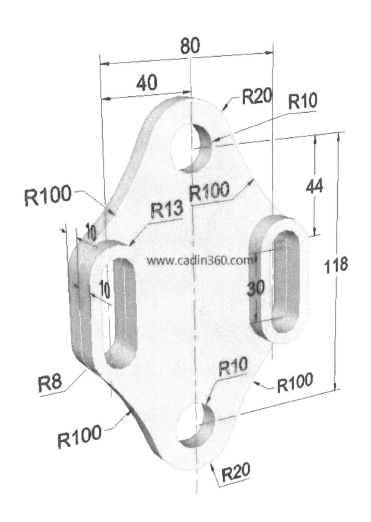

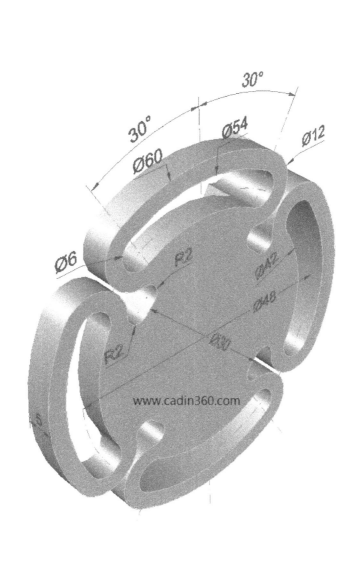

www.cadin360.com

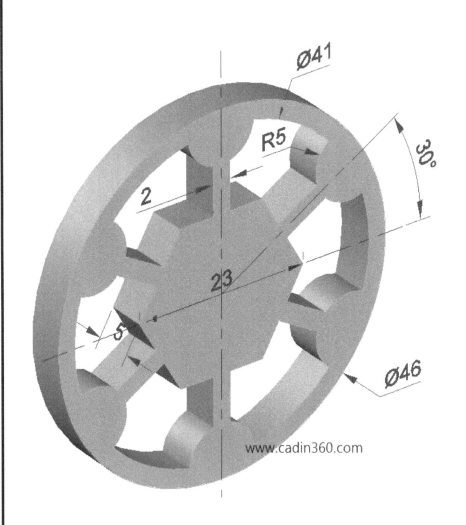

Ø41

R5

2

30°

23

5

Ø46

www.cadin360.com

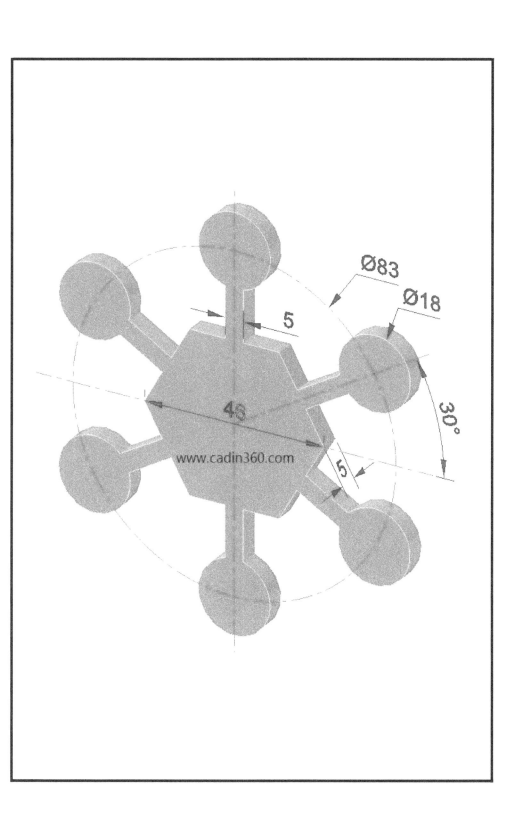

Ø83

Ø18

5

46

30°

5

www.cadin360.com

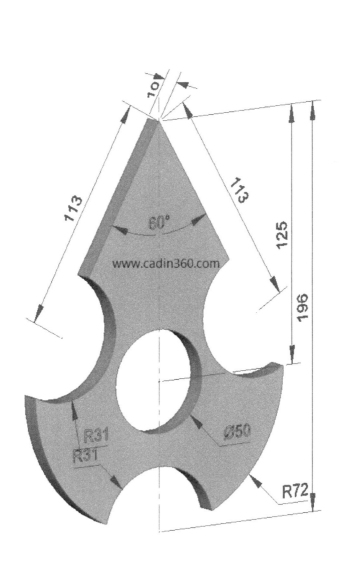

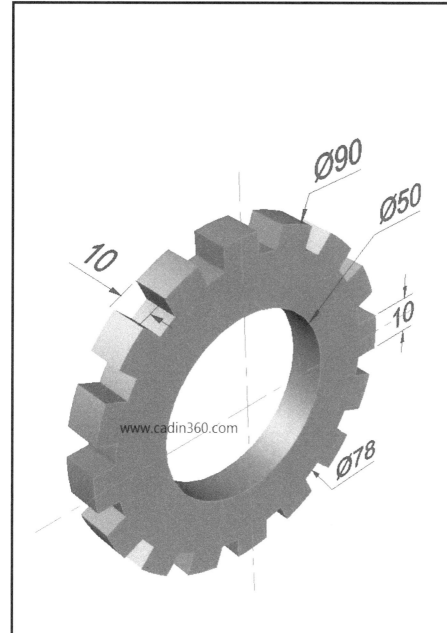

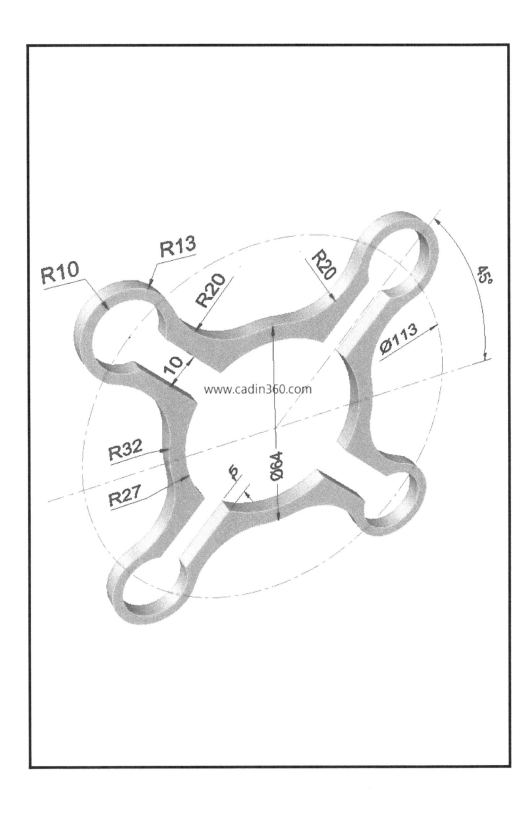

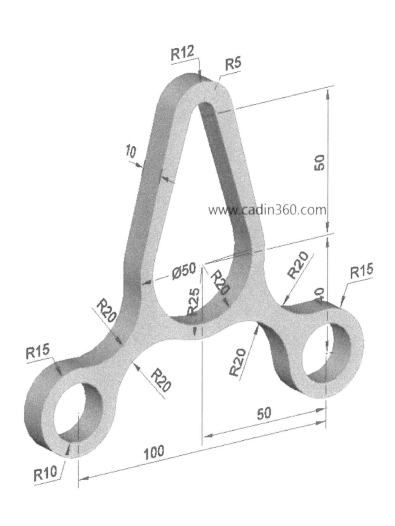

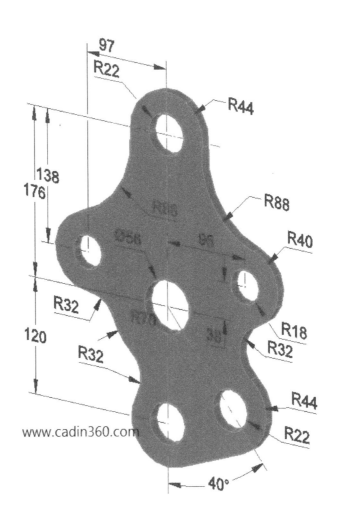

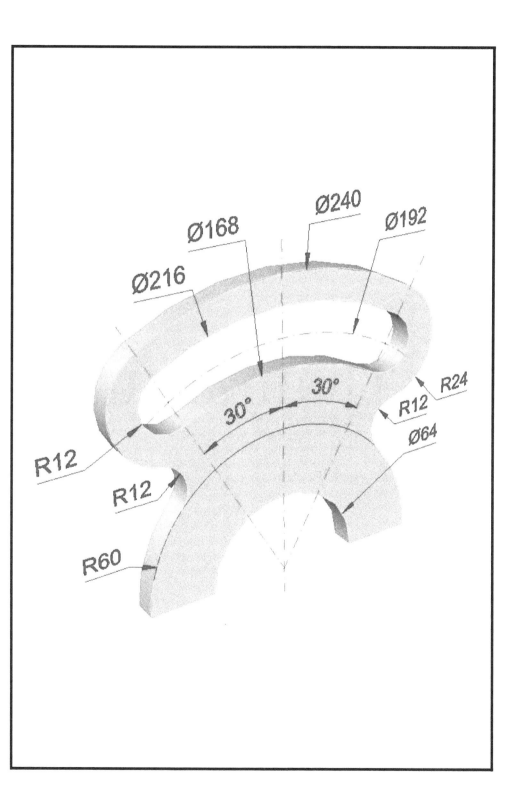

Thank You